77-0900

944.36   Shaw, Irwin
SHA
         Paris! Paris!

DATE			

G

1—

7-8 92

Paris! Paris!

Hurrah for St Trinian's

The Female Approach

Back to the Slaughterhouse

The Terror of St Trinian's

Down with Skool

How to be Topp

Whizz for Atomms

Back in the Jug Agane

The Compleet Molesworth

Souls in Torment

Merrie England, Etc.

The Rake's Progress

Which Way Did He Go?

Looking at London

Paris Sketchbook

From Frozen North to Filthy Lucre

Pardong M'sieur

Searle's Cats

By Rocking Chair Across America

By Rocking Chair Across Russia

Take One Toad

The Square Egg and the Vicious Circle

Refugees 1960

The Big City

Haven't We Met Before Somewhere?

Searle in the Sixties

The Penguin Ronald Searle

The St Trinian's Story

Those Magnificent Men in Their Flying Machines

The Addict

More Cats

Dick Deadeye

by IRWIN SHAW
and RONALD SEARLE

HARCOURT BRACE JOVANOVICH   New York and London

Library of Congress Cataloging in Publication Data

Shaw, Irwin, 1913-
   Paris! Paris!

   1. Paris—Description. 2. Shaw, Irwin, 1913-
—Homes and haunts—France—Paris. I. Searle, Ronald,
1920-   II. Title.
DC707.S47   944′.36′0820924   76-27415
ISBN 0-15-170968-8

First edition

B C D E

Some of the chapters in this book have been published before
in slightly altered versions.

FOR TONY
whose idea it was

Contents

The form for this book was suggested by the late Tony Godwin. In working it out it was decided that the writer and the artist would go about their tasks separately, with no direct collaboration between them. In the event, Mr. Searle never read my text until he had submitted his drawings, and I had never spoken to him about his contribution until his drawings had been mailed from his home in France to New York. The result is a double view of Paris, not in any way an illustration of the text.

I. S.

Preface

This volume is not an autobiographical one, although, as will be seen, bits and pieces of autobiographical material inevitably have crept in. It is not meant to explain the Parisians, either to themselves or to anybody else—except perhaps to myself. Perhaps in the end it has helped me to understand why I spent the best part of a quarter of a century in a country that was not my own.

*L*IKE all affairs, my affair with Paris has gone through many stages. It began in Brooklyn when I was about eleven. At that age I decided that I was going to be a writer or perish in the attempt. A similar attraction must have been felt by other would-be writers or painters all over America, perhaps at an earlier birthday, certainly as they approached their twenties. It may have started with the reading of Dumas or Théophile Gautier or Balzac or a book by Fitzgerald or by seeing a movie about fighter pilots in World War I, or just by sensing something in the general climate of the time that made one feel that no artist could consider himself fully prepared for his life-work without eating a croissant for breakfast in the capital of France or having a *fine* at the Dôme.

As I grew older my appetite for the unseen city was whetted by the tales of returning travelers. A young instructor at my college told me how he had picked up a copy of *Ulysses* in a Parisian bookstore and had lain on his bed in a cheap hotel near Saint-Germain-des-Prés for twenty-eight hours without sleep, food, or drink reading the book until he had come to the last thunderous "Yes."

The instructor was Irish, and *Ulysses* was not yet allowed into Puritan America. The combination seemed to prove something magical and all-embracing about the city. Later, a Russian friend of mine, a painter, who had immigrated to America after a period in Paris, recounted how he had paid for his meals, hotels, and occasionally girls with his canvases. A theatrical director who put on several of my plays had earned his doctorate at the Sorbonne and regaled me with accounts of every play he had seen in Paris, every concert he had listened to, and every art gallery he had visited. A. J. Liebling, whom Harold Ross of *The New Yorker* dubbed The Frog Lover and who was a devoted gourmet, made my mouth water merely by reciting the menus of the meals he had consumed in various out-of-the-way bistros.

This was all before the war, and everybody was young and all these people seemed to speak French and to have had the best times of their lives in Paris and urged me to see for myself, and each year I promised myself, this spring I shall go, or this summer.

Yet when I finally did settle down to live there, I was well over thirty and it came about by accident. I had been there during World War II, briefly, but that was not the same thing, although even then I managed to sit at a table on the *terrasse* of the Dôme and visit the small bar in the back of the Ritz, helmeted and carrying a carbine.

The accident occurred in the summer of 1951 when I came over to France on the *Liberté* with my wife and one-year-old son and took a house on the Cap d'Antibes for two months. We had tickets to return to New York on the thirtieth of September and fully intended to do so. But just as we were packing to leave the Côte d'Azur for a short tour of France that was to end in Cherbourg, where we were to board ship, I met an American couple who had been living in Paris for several years and were on their way back to the United States on business for two or three months. They suggested we take over their apartment on the Rue du Boccador, near the Avenue George V, until they got back, and the offer set all the old Brooklyn literary juices going again. We had only to pay the rent, which was seventy-five dollars a month, a sum which at that time was well within my means, and they would give us ample warning as to when we would have to move out. Sight unseen I agreed and notified the French Line that we were canceling our reservations on that particular voyage, although we were keeping our tickets for a later crossing.

One year later I finally got my money back from the French Line and subleased my apartment in New York. Two years later I gave up the apartment for good and put all the furniture in storage. In the end I have not yet returned to New York, except to visit, and the American couple has never come back to Paris.

Almost twenty-five years later, another real estate accident has finally removed me from Paris. My landlady (whom I paid considerably more than seventy-five dollars a month for a much smaller apartment than the one on the Rue du Boccador) unexpectedly told me that I would have to move out, using the usual French gambit for getting rid of tenants—she explained that her son was getting married and that he needed the place. As far as I can tell, this is practically the only way to get a tenant out of a building without going into endless Gallic litigation. The French are very finicky about property rights, and possession of the premises is a solemn business and not to be disregarded lightly. For example, no one, no matter how delinquent he is, can be expelled from a rented apartment in the cold months between December and April. I know all this and perhaps could have held on for years with a clever lawyer, but I am a superstitious man and felt that the landlady's request was an omen that the time had come to move on, and I raised no objections. The number of Americans was rapidly falling in France anyway, for several reasons, chief among which was the disastrous rate of the dollar against the franc, plus the feeling that France was sliding into a political and economic crisis that would make living there considerably less agreeable than it had been in the halcyon days of the fifties. I decided in the course of the landlady's twenty-minute visit that I had no wish to be left stranded, a last, desolate, trans-Atlantic monument to a joyous invasion that had come and gone.

I felt no particular sentimental throbbing as I packed my things and prepared to decamp. Although the neighborhood in which the building is situated is a lively and agreeable one on the Left Bank, the apartment itself was small and modern and meanly designed, even though it had a terrace from which you could see the top of the Eiffel Tower if you looked in the right direction. Eight guests made it seem terribly crowded, and no more than four people could sit down to dinner in it at the same time.

By contrast, my first apartment, although it was flimsily furnished, not particularly spacious, and situated in a building that had been allowed to run down during the war and in the harsh days after it, had the capacity to welcome as many friends as anybody wanted to see at any one time. Since the building also housed Teddy White, later to become the Homer of the American

Presidency, Art Buchwald, and Félicien Marceau, playwright and novelist who is now a member of the Académie Française, as well as Raoul Lévy, the movie producer who, with Roger Vadim, was the father of cinematic soft porn and who, for the first glorious time, gave us Brigitte Bardot, naked, in *Dieu Créa La Femme,* I did not have to go far for spirited company. Everybody brought everybody else's guests home, and there was a lively flow of newspapermen, visiting novelists, French starlets, movie directors, photographers who had just returned from some distant catastrophe, jockeys, chess players, aspiring Ivy League writers who later turned out to be CIA agents but who didn't let it spoil their fun, and ingenious and worthwhile freeloaders who wanted to be where the drinks were, all coming up the wheezy little elevator, the jubilation of their arrival noisy three floors down.

The elevator was a bone of contention between the tenants of the building and the two old ladies who owned it and their nephew, who managed it. You could do anything you wanted in the building, and I have the feeling that some of us did, without complaint from the trio; you could *rise* in the elevator, but you were warned not to *descend* in it. It had something to do with rent controls, the cost of electricity, and sheer, congenital thrift. The two ladies, dressed in black, and their nephew, who looked like a butcher in the Auvergne, would make spot checks when they heard the sorrowful creaking of the cables in the elevator shaft, and woe to the unwary traveler who was caught descending in the gloomy little cage. Threats of lawsuits and evictions were among the milder forms of reprimand. Delivery boys, moving men, and other members of the working class who might be carrying anything larger than a tennis bag were not allowed even to ascend, and one of the loudest moments in the dim hallways came when a poor, rebellious, bent old man was intercepted trying to sneak two kitchen chairs up to the sixth floor.

But the nephew, perhaps in an effort to prove that gallantry was not dead in France, made a gesture of such delicacy on one memorable, mechanized descent that I remember it to this day. My wife and I boldly got into the elevator on the third floor and started down. The nephew was waiting for us, livid, on the ground floor and began his usual tirade.

"Monsieur," I said, "will you kindly notice the condition of my wife's leg."

My wife had broken her leg skiing and it was in a cast above the knee. The nephew stopped in midsentence and slowly looked down. "Ah, pardon, madame," he said and tipped his hat—to the cast.

The next week he told me he had to raise the rent. When I told him I objected to this, he said that he would have recourse to a lawyer. I countered this by saying I would also be represented by a lawyer. He nodded reasonably, approving my choice of weapons. "If our lawyers reach a satisfactory compromise," he said, "I shall ask you to do me the honor of signing a copy of one of your books."

In the event, the lawyers did not reach a satisfactory compromise. I never signed his book, and we moved to another part of town, in a building without an elevator.

I bear the nephew and his black-garbed aunts no ill will. The time I spent as their tenant was even better than I had expected it to be, and I don't know whether the high point came on the night of a loudly applauded opening of a play of mine, winningly acted by a zestful young French company, or when I gave the wedding party for Art Buchwald and his bride and everybody who could cram into the apartment crammed.

Later on I lived in many parts of Paris, on the Ile Saint-Louis, in Neuilly, in the sixteenth arrondissement, on the Left Bank, in Auteuil. Some of the places were impressively luxurious, others not, but it was never like the first years, and I suppose it couldn't be. Still, all in all, the more than two decades slipped by with more pleasure than pain. If I had been a Parisian, responsible for my government and aghast at many of the things that went on in the city, I imagine the ratio of pain to pleasure might have been reversed. But I was never a Parisian. I was always an American, on an extended visit to be sure, who roamed the streets of the city fondly, dined in some of the great houses and in some that were not so great, listened to the gossip and mingled happily with the natives, working with theater people, editors, movie crews, most often in harmony and admiration. Somehow, all during the period when almost every wall was decorated with the sign, "Americans Go Home," it never occurred to me that they meant me.

Arrival

*T*HE first time I saw Paris was on the day of its liberation, August 25, 1944.

I was in a Signal Corps camera unit that was attached to the Twelfth Regiment of the Fourth Division. The unit was made up of two cameramen, a driver, and myself, all of us privates or Pfc's. Our jeep was banked with flowers, a gift from the people in the little towns on our route to Paris, and we had a small store of tomatoes and apples and bottles of wine that had been tossed to us as we slowly made our way through the crowds that tore down barricades in our path. As we came to a halt in the square before Notre Dame, a boy in the truck ahead of us looked up at the spires and said wonderingly, "And one month ago I was in Bensonhurst."

German prisoners kept going by in droves, in the custody of grinning F.F.I. men, but aside from receiving a few loud, juicy insults from livelier members of the crowds that seemed to flood every street in Paris and having to submit to hearing the "Marseillaise" sung fifteen times an hour, they were not harmed. Among the prisoners, there were many high-ranking officers of the Paris garrison, in pretty uniforms and trying to walk slowly and appear dignified. They were having a hard time of it. It is much easier to appear dignified when surrendering to soldiers in the presence of other soldiers than in the middle of a city full of voluble, newly liberated citizens, mostly women, who have hated you for four years and who spend half their time kissing your conquerors and the other half devising means of breaking through the ranks and taking a quick swipe at the highest officer in your column.

From the direction of the Opéra came the sudden sound of artillery fire. You grew to feel that the sound of guns was quite natural and right in the country, but it always seemed heavy and ominous and strange in a city, especially one bedecked with flags and whose entire population seemed to be on the streets celebrating. We drove up the right bank of the Seine toward the sound of the firing. The streets suddenly were empty, and somewhere, between one block and another, the holiday was ended and the war rebegun.

We stopped our jeep near the Louvre. Leaving the driver and one cameraman there, the other cameraman— Pfc Philip Drell, of Chicago—and I went on foot toward the Rue de Rivoli. Some tanks of the Second French Armored Division were attacking the Ministry of the Navy, at the far end of the Rue de Rivoli, and now and then answering machine-gun fire swept down the long, open, empty boulevard. At each street intersection hundreds of Parisians stood in little groups behind the protection of the buildings. Occasionally a braver or more curious member of the crowd would dart out for a quick look at the action at the end of the street and come back and report, and one gentleman established himself on the sidewalk behind a very slender lamppost, which he obviously felt afforded him cover, and kept a pair of binoculars trained on the contest, oblivious of the bullets that whizzed past him. Several French jeeps sped by and were applauded as they passed each intersection, much the way a favorite pitcher is applauded as he comes in from the bullpen to relieve a faltering teammate in a tight spot at Yankee Stadium.

Hugging the sides of the buildings, Drell and I made our way to a store that had been converted into an F.F.I. first-aid station. There was desultory sniping in the back streets in the neighborhood, and F.F.I. volunteer nurses, carrying bloody litters, kept swooping out onto the bullet-swept Rue de Rivoli to bring back wounded. Dressed in long white smocks, waving large white flags with red crosses on them, running in an awkward, crowded, up-and-down, womanly way, they looked like a group of distracted sea gulls as they rushed back and forth. A wounded German was marched down the street by two cocky F.F.I. boys. The German had been hit in the side, and there was a wide, spreading stain of blood on his uniform, and his face was drained and pale, but he some-how made it under his own power to the door of the aid station. A Senegalese, who had been fighting a private war of his own up a back street, came through the crowd with a shattered hand streaming blood, dragging his rifle in his good hand, an abstracted, absent expression on his face as he stared at his wound.

Abruptly one of the tanks that had been firing at the sandbagged Ministry broke off, turned, and raced at top speed, lurching from side to side, its engine roaring, its treads sparking, down toward us. As it approached each intersection, there was the inevitable hearty round of applause, which suddenly stopped dead as soon as the tank had passed. The top of the tank was open and the tank commander was half out of the hatch, his face gaunt and strained, his eyes wildly staring straight ahead. As he passed us, some of the people around us started to applaud. Then they stopped, too. In the rear plate of the tank there was a large, neat, round hole in the armor, and from the hole a fierce spurt of fire was whipping back. The tank swept crazily down the street and disappeared. I am not sure what happened to it, but the next day a sergeant in command of another tank in the Second French Armored Division told me that one of the tanks in his company had been hit the day before and all five of the crew had been burned to death, and it may have been the one I saw.

There were three or four huge columns of smoke staining the sky in the distance, and I told Drell that I thought we ought to get to a high vantage point from which we could take some pictures. A Frenchman standing in the doorway of the first-aid station overheard me and told us, in English, that he would take us to a good spot. Crouched over, the three of us darted down the Rue de Rivoli and into a side street that was completely empty. "Watch the windows," he warned us. "The snipers keep moving from window to window." We watched the windows with the old, uncomfortable feeling (which you had in any town where there were still snipers) that buildings are made with a ridiculously extravagant number of windows. The Frenchman offered to carry Drell's carbine so that he would have both hands free for his camera. "Ah," the Frenchman said, admiringly fondling the weapon as we walked close to the sides of the buildings, "it is very handsome. So *légère*. Could you give it to me?" We explained that we could not donate carbines at random to the civilian population of France, and he sighed regretfully.

A door opened and a small, bareheaded man with an F.F.I. armband popped out of a building with an arcade in front of it. On one of the pillars of the arcade a red cross had been painted. We ran into the building, and I saw that it was a theater. As we went up the stairs, I saw, too, that the lobby had been transformed into a crude hospital and that there were about thirty wounded lying in litters and on blankets on the floor. Our guide explained that he was an actor and that he had played here. "This is the Comédie Française," he said. He stopped on the steps to impress us further. "It is the greatest theater in France."

"Yes," I said, "I know." Outside, the sound of the fighting grew stronger and I pointed up toward the roof to show him I was impatient to get there. He resumed climbing.

"You don't understand," he said. "It plays the classics of French dramatic literature. The greatest plays in the world." He stopped again to give this explanation.

"Yes," I said, "I know. Let's get to the roof."

We climbed some more, past the busts of the great actors and actresses of France that adorn each landing of the stairway. "You don't understand," he said. "This is the most famous theater in the world." He stopped and lectured me from above. There were several bursts of machine-gun fire about four hundred yards away. "The greatest actors of the modern theater play here . . ."

"Yes, yes, I understand," I said, gently trying to push him upward. "I know all about the Comédie Française. I myself write plays," I said, in an attempt to settle the issue and get to the roof.

"A playwright!" he said, and he beamed with pleasure. "An American playwright! Wonderful!" He shook my hand and started down. "You must come downstairs and meet the artists."

I stopped him. There was a fury of firing outside, as though some new crisis had been reached. "Later," I promised him. "After we take our pictures."

Reluctantly he turned around and led us up to the roof. The roofs of Paris, seen from the top of the

Comédie Française, seemed dangerously bare and quiet. Drell took his pictures with the fussy, lens-adjusting deliberation that is so exasperating in cameramen at moments like that. We were sniped at once as he was finishing, the bullet making a nasty, sudden whistle between us. We went down the steps to the floor below, where it was safe. Drell reloaded his camera, and the Frenchman said of the sniper, "It missed by a good deal. Undoubtedly it was a woman." He was the only man I met in the war who could tell the sex of the firer of a gun by the whistle of the bullet as it passed him.

We started down the stairs again, and the Frenchman looked in at various offices for artists to whom he wished to introduce me. But all the offices were empty. "Ah, they are all downstairs," he said. "There are a lot of wounded."

We went down to the lobby. There was a smell of antiseptic and a slight smell of ether, and under floodlights in one corner of the large, low room, an operation was taking place. Strong beams of sunlight, with the dust dancing in them, broke into the gloom at several places. Half-naked men were being helped toward the doctors, and in a corner lay two bodies wrapped in French flags. Here and there, from one of the men lying on the floor in rows, there came a groan, and the nurses, of whom there were many, trotted busily among them. The nurses, the Frenchman said, were all actresses, most of them from the Comédie Française company. They were very pretty and dressed in light, soft dresses; the effect, with the sharp contrasts of the light and shadow, the white gleam of the wounded bodies, the piles of bloody bandages, the two dead men in the flags, and the pretty young girls carrying basins and morphine syringes, was that of a painting by Goya for whom the models had been picked by Samuel Goldwyn.

Everybody was very busy, and I told our guide that the introductions could wait for another day. A tall, gray-haired man with his sleeves rolled up, who seemed to be in charge, came over and asked, "Are you Americans?"

"Yes," I said.

"Please come with me," he said. He took me by the arm and led me over to the corner where the dead were lying. He bent over and pulled back the flags. The dead were in OD's and had been recently killed. One of them was a very young blond boy who had been shot through the temple—a small, exact, round wound from which the blood still seeped out onto the stone floor under his thin, handsome, sunburned, healthy-looking face.

"Are they Americans or French?" the gray-haired man asked me.

I looked. Both the dead were wearing the little enamel badge of the French Army (which had not been seen in Paris until that day) over their right breasts. "French," I said.

The gray-haired man put his hand under the blond boy's armpits and half picked him up and shook him very roughly. "You're all right, *mon copain*," he said, almost smiling. "You're all right." He shook him again and again like a man joking roughly with an old friend in a barracks room. "You're all right." He let the dead boy drop to the floor, smacked him vigorously and almost vulgarly on the shoulder, as though he refused to admit the fact of death, and turned away to his work. I stood looking for a moment at the blond boy and the hole in his temple. He had a streak of rouge on his cheek, like all the soldiers in Paris that day, and there was a dark wine stain down the front of his khaki wool shirt.

Drell and I made our way back toward the Rue de Rivoli. The firing had stopped and we walked down the middle of the street. From all the side streets, thousands of people, seeing us walking unharmed and taking it as a signal of victory, flocked out, applauding, cheering, kissing us, men and women alike, indiscriminately. Of all the hundreds of people who kissed me that day, including, I imagine, some very pretty girls, I remember most clearly a small, fat, middle-aged man—one of the few fat men I saw in Paris—who held me close and kissed me with all the fervor of a husband returned to a loved wife after five years of war.

The smell of perfume from the crowd, now so closely packed in the street down which fifteen minutes before the doomed tank had wavered, was overpoweringly strong, and the variety of rich, sweet odors, as kiss followed kiss, was dazzling and unreal to a soldier who had been living in the field, in mud and dust, for two months. One slender, sharp-eyed woman came up to me and touched my shoulder affectionately but appraisingly, like the man who guessed your weight at Coney Island. "Ah," she said, smiling pleasantly and without envy, satisfied now by touch as well as by sight that I was really as large as I looked, "ah, you have eaten well."

The driver and the other cameraman were waiting with the jeep. They looked very neat and clean, and their hair had been combed. "What happened to you?" I asked.

"An old lady came out of one of the buildings," the

driver said, "and looked at us and said, 'You're awfully dirty,' and went in and came back with a basin and pitcher of water and a cake of soap and a towel and made us wash ourselves. Then she went away."

We drove slowly through the swarming crowds, over broken glass, past still-burning German tanks of the recent battlefield, to the Place de la Concorde, now filling with people. A thin, fair little woman and her husband came over to me. The woman said she was American, born in Syracuse. Her husband was French and she had been in Paris throughout the Occupation. Her eyes were shining and she and her husband kept smiling widely, no matter what the conversation was about. "You're the first American soldier I've seen," she said and started to lean over to kiss my cheek. Then she checked herself and turned to her husband. "May I kiss him?" she asked, a little doubtfully. "Certainly," the husband said gravely. She kissed me on both cheeks.

Suddenly, in the little grove of trees at the end of the Place de la Concorde near the bridge across the Seine, we saw the puffs of explosions, mortar shells bursting at regular intervals. The great square emptied quickly, except for the inevitable F.F.I. Red Cross workers, who ran, swooping, toward the trees. Some French tanks took up position along the river, and one of them, at the approach to the bridge that leads directly to the steps of the Chambre des Députés on the Left Bank, began to fire sporadically into the huge, pillared building. Some F.F.I. riflemen appeared and took cover behind the balustrade along the river and added their fire to that of the tank. A rickety old truck, with an open, wooden body filled with F.F.I. men who had mounted a thirty-caliber machine gun in makeshift fashion, drove furiously to one side of the square and stopped under a slender little tree, which I suppose the driver imagined concealed them completely. All the F.F.I. men except the machine gunner dropped off and hid behind the monuments with which the Place de la Concorde had been thoughtfully provided. The gunner stood up at his weapon and let loose a fierce, uninterrupted stream of bullets across the river at the august side of the Chambre des Députés. The calmer heads among his comrades recognized the wastefulness of this one-man barrage against thick stone walls and began to group around him, remonstrating. He kept firing with one hand and waving them away with the other, arguing bitterly, until three of them jumped onto the truck, dragged him off, and installed a more conservative machine gunner.

A jeep drove slowly up to the tank, which was still firing, and a young French lieutenant got out and stood, motionless and arrogantly exposed, next to it, directing its fire. It was quite brave of him, because the mortar fire was dropping unpredictably; he was the sort of lieutenant any soldier crouched behind cover remembers and hates. A nondescript collection of people had taken shelter behind the great stone block at the approach to the bridge, including four or five unarmed members of the F.F.I. and a young girl in a white dress who was holding a bicycle. Off to the right, on our bank of the Seine, a pretty little yacht, which Renoir might have used as a model for his river-outing paintings, burned brightly. A German prisoner was brought up and placed, with a large white flag, on the tank. A French officer took up a position ahead of the tank, and Drell left me to join him. The tank started across the bridge, with the prisoner waving the flag frantically and the officer and Drell walking ahead of it, to demand the surrender of the Germans in the Chambre des Députés. The mortar shells started up again, first hitting in the river, then finding the bridge, finally breaking off a lamppost and wounding several people five yards from the protecting stone block. The officer pulled the German prisoner off the tank, and he and the officer and Drell ran across the bridge to the other side while the tank moved back. The three of them stood there in front of the Chambre des Députés, the prisoner monotonously waving his flag while the mortar fire continued for another ten minutes, roaming along the bridge. Then I saw Drell and the Frenchman run up the steps of the Chambre des Députés and disappear into it. I moved about fifty yards upstream, to where an F.F.I. man was firing his rifle six times á minute at the un-responding official architecture on the other side of the river. A French tank was in position there, its gun trained on the Chambre but not firing. The hatch was open, and a tough, curly-haired French tankman was standing up in it, completely exposed, staring at himself in a small pocket mirror. He noticed me eying him from down below. He shrugged. *"C'est bizarre, n'est-ce pas?"* he said and turned back to admiring himself in the mirror.

Every once in a while a bullet passed over our heads, but an old sedan loaded with F.F.I. men was able to dash unmolested across the bridge, and I followed on foot. When I got to the Chambre des Députés, I found that the three or four hundred Germans there had just surrendered. Drell and the French officer had become separated, and the Germans had tried to surrender to Drell, who was unarmed except for his camera, but American. Drell insisted that he couldn't accept the surrender and got the Germans to agree to let him take pictures of them surrendering to the French. Negotiations were carried out, on Drell's part in Yiddish, the nearest thing to a common tongue he and the Germans could find.

After the surrender, the Germans drew up in ranks in the courtyard, their arms stacked at one side. (They had left a shambles inside the handsome rooms—a deep litter of sardine tins, used cartridges, biscuit boxes, and empty champagne bottles all over the regal red plush.) A lot of correspondents and photographers had arrived, and the scramble for souvenirs was lively. Suddenly we heard the sound of a shell approaching, the sickening, unmistakable whistle of a shell that is going to land right near you. We all hit the gravel, face down, trying in the awful, traditional way to burrow into the earth even one-quarter of an inch before the explosion found us. The noise of the approaching shell grew louder and louder, keeping up for an interminably long time, longer than any artillery sound I had ever heard before. I lay there with the certainty that this was the one that was going to land directly on the exposed back of my neck. Then the noise suddenly stopped. There was no explosion. After a moment I looked up. All the French and all the Americans were on the ground, fingers and faces deep in the gravel, and all the prisoners were standing absolutely erect, laughing. Every outfit in every army has a mimic who can produce the most deadly, realistic whistle of an approaching shell through his teeth. The captured Germans were no exception, and the comedian had just put on the most successful performance of his career. Drell and I got up sheepishly, dusted ourselves off, collected our loot—Lugers, belts, cameras, and a bicycle—and made our way back to our jeep, where the other cameraman, a very handsome twenty-year-old boy with a deep South

Carolina accent, was happily jotting down the addresses of three or four dozen girls who were grouped around the jeep.

We drove off, with a cluster of girls hanging onto the jeep, and found the Hôtel Scribe, where we had been told to report with our film. Outside the hotel, inundating the army vehicles there, were hundreds of Parisians, singing, shaking hands, asking questions, examining jeeps and guns, extending invitations, weeping, kissing the soldiers, kissing the correspondents, kissing each other.

As we were unloading our jeep, a Frenchman came up to me and shook my hand. He was dressed with painful neatness in old, threadbare clothes, and he seemed more shaken than exhilarated by the events of the day.

"How long does it take a letter to get to the United States?" he asked me in heavily accented English.

"About ten days," I said.

"Where do you live?" he asked.

"New York," I told him.

"I have a sister in Brooklyn," he said. "I have not seen her for nine years. She has not heard from me in four years." He looked around nervously, leaned over, and spoke in a whisper. "I am a Jew. I wonder if it is possible for you to write her for me through your mails."

"Certainly," I said, and I wrote down the address of his sister in Brooklyn. "Now," I said, "what do you want to tell her?"

He looked at me a little dazedly, as though stunned and frightened by the magnitude of the opportunity being presented to him. He stared around him at the celebrating girls and wrinkled his brow, concentrating intensely.

"Tell her," he said, "tell her I'm alive." He shook my hand and went off.

Drell and I went into the hotel and grandly registered for two large rooms, knowing that the day of the Pfc in Paris would be short and determined to make the most of it. There was no hot water, but I luxuriated in the bath nevertheless, listening to the voice of the crowd down below, an endless swelling mixture of cheers, song, and high, feminine laughter. As I lay there, washing off the grit and heat of the long day, listening to the celebrating crowd on the streets below, it was possible to feel that a new age of courage, decency, and gratitude was beginning in Europe.

Just before I fell asleep I remembered what I had heard a GI say that momentous afternoon: "This is the day the war should end."

Searle's Paris: 1

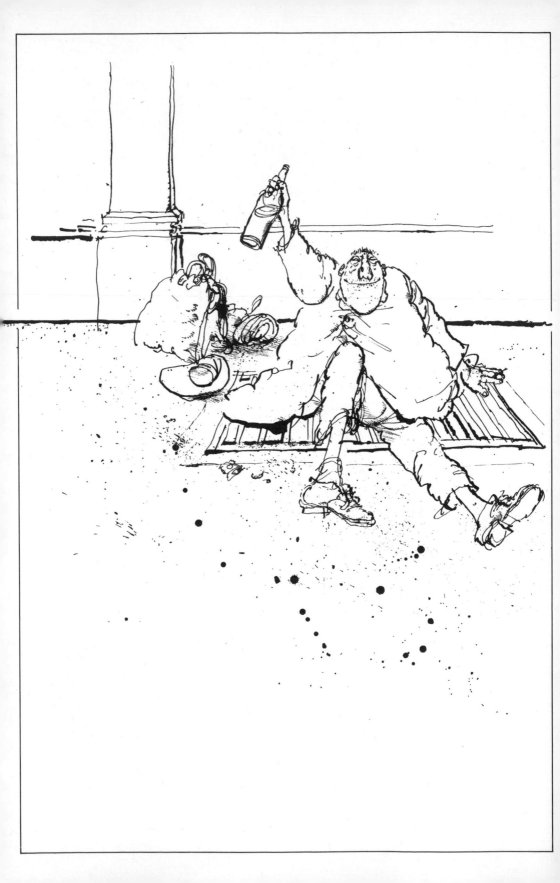

Remembrance of Things Past

A piece about the Paris of more than twenty years ago is bound to be an evocation of a time that, like Proust's prewar city, has slipped into the mist, where maps are no longer reliable, streets unfamiliar, beauties recalled in a sigh, giants gone.

When the following piece was written in the mid-nineteen fifties, I entitled it simply "Paris." But the editors at *Holiday* magazine, themselves young men at that period and thriving in the exuberant years when American arms had won the war and American money was restoring the world, made it "Paris! Paris!," the double exclamation demonstrating their jaunty belief in the city of light three thousand miles away, which most of them had never visited.

*Y*OU start at a café table because everything in Paris starts at a café table. You are waiting for the girl you love.

She is young and American and perfect. She has straight legs and an enormous appetite and solid low-heeled shoes and she likes to walk and she has just arrived in the city for the first time in her life and she likes to listen to you talk and she is imaginary. She is late, of course, because you have been so conditioned by the women you have known that even the ones you invent can't meet you on time. You have invented her because you have been daydreaming; you have been playing with the idea of pleasure, and it has occurred to you that there could be few things more pleasurable in this sad world than to roam Paris for a day hand in hand with such a girl.

You sit there, glowing with the prospect of unfolding Paris for the first time to this superb, unreal, and uninitiated creature.

It is summer or autumn or winter or spring and it is sunny and raining and there is snow on the statues and bits of ice in the Seine and the trees are all in full blossom and the swimmers are diving into the purified water in the wooden pools along the river banks and it is early in the morning and late at night and the President is giving a ball and the Garde Républicaine is out in breastplates and horsehair tails and the North Africans are rioting for autonomy at the Place de la République and all the policemen have dents in their shining steel helmets.

Mass is being celebrated at Saint-Sulpice and they are burying an actor in Père Lachaise. There are long lines outside the mail windows at the American Express. The young lieutenants are leaving for Indochina. There is a fair on the Esplanade des Invalides and the phrenologists are doing well next to the shooting galleries. They are selling perfume on the Rue de la Paix and the wine merchants are worried about this year's Burgundy and a thousand deep baskets of watercress are being stacked at Les Halles. The buses are coming in from Orly airfield to the Gare des Invalides with the passengers from New York and South Africa and Warsaw and the trains going south have whole cars filled with bicycles for the vacationers en route to the Côte d'Azur. It is August and half the shops are closed, with their iron shutters down, and it is February and the porters wait with wheelchairs at the Gare de l'Est for the skiers with broken legs.

On the gray islands in the river they are turning out four hundred fifty buglike, four-horsepower Renaults a day and the Communists are painting "Americans Go

Home'' on the iron bridges. They are selling canaries near the Hôtel de Ville and putting out newspapers on the Rue Réaumur and the headlines show that the Premier is worried about the price of butter, that French football has suffered another catastrophe at Colombes, and that a young woman with an Algerian lover has walled up her landlady in the cellar. The butchers are putting lilacs in their windows and everybody at the flea market is guaranteeing that everything is over a hundred years old. A carousel calliope is playing under the elevated structure on the Boulevard Garibaldi and children are getting rides in goat carts near the American Embassy. There is a new middleweight fighting at the Palais des Sports who will never make anyone forget Marcel Cerdan. A pensioner has committed suicide because he was afraid the inflation would deprive him of his tobacco and there is a banquet planned for the millers who are accused of driving a whole town mad with flour tainted by ergot, the event organized by the flour manufacturers who wanted to demonstrate their solidarity with their unlucky colleagues.

It is Sunday and the couples are sprawled all over the Bois and the lions are roaring for the crowds across the deep moats in the Vincennes zoo. It is the fourteenth of July, and there are parades and the placing of wreaths in the memory of the dead and the memory of the Bastille and the memory of the unfortunate Foullon, whose head was carried on a pike up the Rue Saint-Martin in 1789, his mouth stuffed with grass because he had said of the people of Paris, ''*Eh bien.* If this riffraff has no bread, they'll eat hay.'' There is also the sound of jets flying in formation over the city, and there is dancing in the streets and in the gardens of the great houses, and there are fireworks in the sky behind the cathedral and marshals of France standing at attention while the bands play the anthem, whose words include, "To arms, citizens!"

It is a workday, and the open platforms of the buses are crowded with people who breathe deeply of the gasoline fumes on their way to their offices. It is market day, and the housewives push through the stalls under the trees at the Place de l'Alma, next to the Salon Nautique, looking at the prices of the chickens and the cheeses and the celery root and complaining that life is too expensive.

There is a smell of freshly baked bread in the air and the streets are full of people hurrying home with long, unwrapped loaves under their arms. In the crowded *charcuteries* there are a dozen different kinds of pâté on the counters and Alsatian *choucroute* and *gnocchi* and snails and *coquilles Saint-Jacques,* ready to be put into the oven, and the salesgirls sound like a cageful of flutes as they call out the prices to the customers. In the Métro there is an experimental train that runs on rubber tires, to alleviate the nervous agony of being alive in the twentieth century. In the Berlitz classrooms the activities of the family Dupont are carefully followed as they say good morning to each other, open and close doors, and lay various objects on a table. On the Ile Saint-Louis the owner of an American convertible finds its top slashed for the seventh time and decides he will have to buy a closed car.

In the lobbies of the big hotels, sharp-eyed men are whispering to each other, making deals to import and export vital materials, and an American at the bar of the George V says to his business associates, "I don't like to boast, but I am very close to the Virginia tobacco industry."

The all-girl orchestras are tuning up for their afternoon programs of waltzes in the big, bare cafés on the Boulevard Clichy, and in the *bals musettes* shopgirls dance with clerks under the paintings of thugs and apaches. There are thousands of people lined up at the Porte Saint-Cloud to watch a bicycle race, and everybody is going to Deauville for the weekend.

The fountains are playing at the Rond-Point, casting a fine spray over the flower borders, and Notre Dame is illuminated and looks as light as a dream on its stone island, and the streets are empty and the traffic heavy, and you sit there planning this limitless, all-seasoned, perfect day with your perfect girl in the city that is the Jerusalem of many strange pilgrimages and the capital of nostalgia and that you can never leave without tasting a faint, bitter flavor of exile.

You sit at the table on land that has been rented from the municipality for four thousand francs a square meter a year, and you remember that there is a rumor that the government, in a typically indirect and tactful attempt to limit alcoholism, is going to raise the price of its sidewalks to make drinking less general or at least more expensive. You are sipping a Cinzano because gin is so dear and it is too early for brandy. Behind you, on the wall of the café, there is a yellowed copy of the law to suppress public drunkenness. The law was passed during World War I but is still in effect, and you admire the men who could worry about things like that with Germans only a few miles away and dropping shells every twenty minutes into the city from the long-range gun that they called Big Bertha and that was trained on Paris from the Saint-Gobain Forest, eighty-two miles distant.

You lift your eyes above the rim of your glass and

read that anyone who is found for the first time in a state of manifest drunkenness in the streets, roads, cafés, cabarets, or other public places can be fined between one and five francs, which at the present rate would range between one-quarter of a cent and a penny. But if you get caught manifestly drunk twice, the results, according to the proclamation, promise to be more grave: For two years you lose the right to vote, the right to serve as a juror or in the administration of the government, and the right to carry arms, and you are deprived, according to the small print, of your paternal powers over your children and your descendants.

You sip soberly at your drink and peer out at the passers-by for the bright American head that is bound to look a little artless and unpremeditated among the clever, artificially streaked short hair of the Parisian women on the boulevard. The girl you love has not yet arrived, and you half-close your eyes and plan the first step.

First, there should be a general, bird's-eye view of the city, and the best place for that is the top of the Eiffel Tower. From there, the city lies embraced by its winding river and flows in a silvery haze over its moderate hills and its central plain. You can look out over the homes and the shops and the cemeteries and places of worship of three million people, and you can see the hill in Montmartre where the Temple of Mercury used to stand and where Saint-Denis was beheaded. You can trace the course of the river and see where the canals join it and the Marne, and you can tell the girl about the Norsemen who sailed up the river in their oared galleys in the ninth century, jovially axing the farmers and the city dwellers along the banks, as was the custom of travelers in that time.

There is one drawback about the tower, though—the elevator makes you nervous. You know that you are unreasonable. You know that since it opened for business in 1889, it has carried millions of people safely up to the top. But you suffer a little from vertigo, and every time you get into the creaking, slightly tilted car you regret, with unreasonable chauvinism, being that high in the air and dependent for your life on French machinery. You would depend unhesitatingly on French courage to get you out of danger, on French medicine to cure a stomach ache, on French wit to make you laugh or a French wife to make you happy—but all that cable, all those girders, all those grinding gears . . . You decide to settle for a more moderate eminence: the top of the Arc de Triomphe is quite high enough for a young girl's first view of Paris, and its elevator is comfortably enclosed in a stone shaft.

Anyway, you will tell her, Paris is not a city of heights. Its architects, out of respect for man, have made certain that man is not dwarfed by his works here. It is a city built to human scale, so that no man should feel pygmied here. Parisians are devoted to their sky and have passed a set of complicated laws designed to keep the height of buildings at a modest level, so that the sky, soft, streaked, gentle, beloved by painters, can be a constant, intimate presence above the roofs and the treetops. In defense of their sky, Parisians can be outlandishly fierce. A builder in Neuilly who put up an apartment house taller than the legal limit was ordered by the court to tear down the top two stories, although they had been leased in advance and there is a crucial housing shortage. In addition, the builder was forced to pay a whopping fine for every day that the offending twenty feet of construction loomed above the skyline. And then, as an aesthetic afterthought, the judge sentenced him to jail. Oh, you think, remembering the caged and distant sky above your native city, if only there were more builders in Sing Sing.

From the top of the monument, staring out at the city, your girl doesn't say anything because she is perfect. The great avenues—which Baron Haussmann, Napoleon III's prefect of police, created to get the mob of Paris out into the open where he could use cavalry on them when they wanted a raise in salary or wished to murder a minister—sweep out to all points of the compass.

The boulevards are named after victories and soldiers, and on the arch itself are the names of one hundred and seventy-two battles chiseled into the stone. Many of the streets of Paris are labeled for battlefields on which Frenchmen have conquered, and you wonder what it must do to the spirit of the citizens of a city to have the sound of triumph on their lips every time they give an address to a taxi driver, and whether they would be different today if, along with the Avenue Wagram and the Avenue de Friedland, there were a Boulevard Sedan, a Rue Waterloo, and a Place of the Surrender.

Although statistically Paris has the least green space per citizen of any major city in Europe, there are so many trees that when they are in foliage and seen from above, much of the metropolis seems to be built in a giant park. Close by, the city leans against the green escarpments of Saint-Cloud and Saint-Germain, across the bending river, reminding you that Paris is more intimate with and more accessible to the countryside than any other great city in the world. The slate, jumbled world of the rooftops is pewter and lavender, Paris's own colors, and there is the gleam of innumerable studio windows, facing north. The pinkish Carrousel past the other end of the Champs Elysées is like a distant and frivolous reflection of the arch on whose peak you are standing, and the wind up here carries a frail leaf-and-mold smell of the river with it. The white dome of the Sacré-Coeur speaks of nineteenth-century religion on the heights of Montmartre, and you can see the gray, medieval stone tower of Saint-Germain-des-Prés rising on the opposite bank from its nest of cafés.

Standing there, with the whole city spread around you, its palaces and spires and statues glistening in the damp sunlight, you reflect aloud to the girl on how wise Parisians are to have had ancestors who were ruled by tyrants, because tyrants are egotists with an itch to build monuments to themselves. Then after a while you get rid of the tyrants and are left with the Louvre and the Tuileries and the obelisk and the Place Vendôme and the brave, sculptured horses and the great boulevards that were built because someone was ruthless enough and powerful enough to tear down acre after acre of people's homes and pave what used to be somebody's kitchen and plant chestnut trees in somebody else's bedroom. You reflect on the selfishness of being alive in your own time. You are delighted with what Louis XIV did to the city with the taxes he squeezed from the poor, and with what Napoleon built on the blood of a generation of young Frenchmen, though you would struggle to the death against a new Louis or a later Napoleon, no matter how many arches and palaces he guaranteed for your descendants to enjoy on their visit from America a hundred years from now.

You remember the first time you climbed to the top of the arch, which was just after the Liberation, when the Twenty-eighth Division marched past to show Paris the Americans were really here. You remember the noise the tanks made on the Champs Elysées, and the massed, weary, pleasant young faces of the soldiers, and the absence of music because they were all going to fight that night at Saint-Denis and they had no time for bands. And you realize that every time you think of the city, there is something of that time in your feeling for it.

It is difficult not to love a city you have seen for the first time on the day it was liberated. And Paris was liberated in just the right way. It hadn't been bombed, except on the outskirts, and all the bridges were still standing, and the inhabitants themselves had spent the last five days firing off small arms and feeling heroic, and the weather was sunny and warm and all the girls wore their best dresses, and there were enough Germans left to put up a show of war and give the local boys an opportunity to behave martially in front of good audiences before the final surrender.

Everybody was thin from the war, but not starving, and you kept hearing the "Marseillaise," and the smoke from a few small fires rose unimportantly here and there, and for an afternoon it felt as though the war had ended and it couldn't have ended in a better place. The word was that von Sholtitz had spared the city, against Hitler's orders, and the Parisians felt, Of course, who could have the heart to blow up Paris? There was blood against some of the walls, and the next day they were piling flowers there for the dead and everybody was kissing everybody else and there was a considerable amount of free wine.

Travelers are always telling you their favorite times for seeing a city for the first time: Rome at Easter, London in June, New York in October, Pittsburgh at five o'clock in the morning. And you tell the girl to make sure to see Paris the next afternoon it is liberated. It is a city that takes gratefully to a mixture of riot, celebration, and bloodshed. The citizens are experts at putting up and tearing down barricades, at killing each other, and at greeting and firing upon troops. The streets are admirably arranged for mass demonstrations, parades, and the maneuvering of armor. The buildings are solid and made of stone and merely chip when hit by shells, and in a year or two the damp, benevolent air ages the scars so that they are indistinguishable from the precious marks of the centuries before. There are monuments everywhere that lend an atmosphere of significance to acts performed in their vicinity, and when people die in front of them in the belief that they are preserving civilization, civilization takes on a tangible and satisfactory presence.

You tell something of this to the girl whose hair is blowing and whose eyes are shining here above the jumble of stone and memory and history, and she squeezes your hand and says, "Isn't it time for lunch? I'm dying."

Then you begin a ritual that is one of the most pleasant in the world—deciding slowly and carefully which place in all the city of Paris is the one place you wish to lunch at that day. You can go to the run-down old hotel on the hill at Saint-Cloud, which has a terrace overlooking some tennis courts, with the river down at the bottom of the slope and the city lost beyond its trees just three hundred yards away on the opposite bank, and you can sit out there getting sunburned, feeding off the tableful of hors d'oeuvre, watching the French play tennis. (The French play a crafty, deft game, slow and full of lobs and chops and angles, and unless you're Sedgman or McGregor, it is less tantalizing to eat lunch and watch them than play against them.) The hotel used to be a club for American airborne officers in the hilarious summer just after the war and cognac used to be ten cents a glass and everybody used to mix it with Coca-Cola and there was a pretty waitress there who decided one night she was wildly in love with an airborne major who weighed a hundred and thirty-five pounds and who was working for the National Broadcasting Company in Chicago the last time you heard about him.

Or, since it is the girl's first day in town and you feel limitlessly wealthy in her presence, you might take a taxi out to the Bois and eat in the restaurant under the glass chandeliers that are swung from the trees and order trout and a bottle of wine and take a walk later and watch the ceremonious ladies and gentlemen cantering around the bridle paths as though nothing had happened since 1900. And you could walk in the forest, which is amazingly like a real forest for a tract of land so close to a large city, and imagine how it must have looked when the troops of Wellington and the Czar were encamped there in 1815 after Napoleon had had his final bad time.

If it is a gray, autumnal day, you can walk on over to Auteuil with her and wander around the almost empty stands and watch the steeplechase races, buying the odds from dusty men in the paddock who have them written down on flimsy strips of yellow paper and putting your bets down, as usual, on the horse that falls at the last hedge, but enjoying the stretching deep green infield and the inconsequent way the horses vanish behind trees, carrying your money with them into obscurity. And you can regret the decline of jump racing in America and the lack of variety in the dirt tracks of Saratoga and Arlington and Santa Anita, where the horses always run the same way, like wooden mounts on a merry-go-round and where your money is always painfully visible as it is being lost.

But if your girl doesn't feel like open air her first afternoon, you can be less enterprising and walk through the eighth, or American, arrondissement, so-called because at certain moments it looks as though the French had moved out and the Americans moved in, and go to a small restaurant that has grapevines planted all along its sliding glass windows, so that everyone is reflected in shimmering green above the tablecloths. It is not your favorite restaurant, but you were witness there to a meal that was not so much a lunch as a ceremony, an act of devotion, a celebration of the mystic nature of food, a reverent wallowing in gluttony that erased for two hours all memory of the drugstore sandwiches and hasty milk shakes of your native land.

The meal was eaten by four grave-faced businessmen, obviously men of importance and economic power, and they started with *pâté de foie gras,* pink and fatty, and went on to *quenelles de brochet*—river fish, flaked and mixed with soaked bread and crumbs, kidney fat, and eggs, and covered with a sauce of mushrooms and cream. The four gentlemen—talking in subdued, polite voices of taxes, labor policies, import difficulties, and the necessity for expanding plants—ate solidly and industriously, washing the *quenelles* down with a half-bottle of Chablis apiece. Then they moved on to slablike Chateaubriands, blue and bloody and complete with fried potatoes and Bordelaise sauce and two bottles of Nuits-Saint-Georges. Then, of course, there was salad and cheese, Brie and Camembert and plump chunks of pale Gruyère, with another bottle of Nuits-Saint-Georges, and fruit and crêpes, flaming with liqueurs, and finally coffee and two brandies apiece, after which they solemnly rose from the table, shook hands, and went back to their offices to oversee the manufacture of automobiles or the transfer of stock.

You walk past the shop where you can buy a silver-handled umbrella for ninety dollars and past the doorway where a ragged, shapeless old lady, wrapped in newspapers, slept all winter, as though she had a lease on the space, past the big hotels where the Hollywood people stay and in front of which the Cadillacs are parked. You go past the corner where a squarely built, rubber-booted, peasantlike flower girl, with bright red cheeks and wearing a fluttering apron, offers lilacs and violets and gladiolas, which she brings each morning in a taxi, whose driver she tips handsomely. You skirt the religious school behind its wall, where the eight-year-old boys arrive bare-legged and chilled each morning and gravely shake hands with each other before going in to their catechism. You walk past the café with the inviting name of La Belle Ferronnière, at whose tables sit the mannequins from the nearby fashion houses, and American soldiers, and a number of Rumanians and Hungarians speaking in their native tongues. The café is dominated by a coffee machine only a little smaller than a locomotive boiler, and the man who tends it leaps from lever to lever and wheel to wheel like a nervous engineer trying to run a dynamo that is slightly out of order. The coffee is black and, contrary to the usual slander, delicious, and if you want it *au lait*, the man behind the counter pours some milk into a copper pitcher and shoots steam into it with a roaring, hoarse noise and serves your coffee frothy and bubbled.

You arrive at the restaurant but the four heroes are not there that afternoon, and you decide to prolong the ecstasy of choosing a place to eat and you saunter down toward the river, and if it is spring the chestnuts are in bloom, pink and white, and even if your girl had never been to Paris before she has read enough about the chestnuts of Paris so that you don't have to say anything about them. But if it is late spring, the blossoms drift thickly along the curbs, swirling up in pink and white clouds with the wind of passing automobiles, and the young girls float across the streets in leafy light and shadow, going to and coming from First Communion in their trailing white veils like frail, light-footed, grave-eyed brides.

Tied up at the stone river banks are the oil barges and the pleasure craft, which can be berthed by payment of a nominal rental to the city and which then can boast what must certainly be the most attractive address in the world, "The River Seine, just a little east of the Pont Alexandre III."

You pass the Grand Palais, where the big exhibitions are held and where the scandal of the Salon d'Automne unfolded, when some propaganda paintings by Communists were hung, then taken down, then hung again, and you remember one in particular, which was called "The Good Health of Comrade Thorez." Comrade Thorez was the head of the French Communist Party; he was in Moscow at the time being treated for a stroke, and the painting showed a band of uniformly smiling workers dancing and registering pleasure while a rosy young woman held up, in the foreground, a newspaper that carried a headline announcing Comrade Thorez's recovery, and it was hard to see whom the picture could damage, except possibly Comrade Thorez, and then only if he were an art critic.

You cross the Pont de la Concorde and stare at the Chambre des Députés. There seem to be dozens of policemen on duty there, in front of the statues, as though the legislators half-expected a rush of citizens to flood past the gates in a berserk desire to vote. Inside, the government is probably falling, and deputies are almost certainly making speeches denouncing each other for their behavior at the time of Munich, or at the signing of the Nazi-Soviet Pact, or during the Occupation, and the Right and the Left are insulting each other and voting together against the government on every proposal. The deputies, in their red-plush amphitheater, do not have the look of ponderous, fleshy well-being of our own congressmen. They seem small, quick, intellectual, and poised for flight, and they have an air of restrained irritation with each other, like passengers in a crowded elevator that has been stuck between floors for a long time. And you remember what a French friend said to you about the then current Premier. "If that man is to be a success," he said, "he must make the French eat worse next year. Anyone can demand austerity in England and get away with it. But in France it takes character."

It was in this chamber that Clemenceau, when he was Premier, came out with one of the most invigoratingly candid statements ever pronounced by the head of a state. "I am against all governments," he growled, "including my own."

You wonder how far the old man would have gotten in an American election with talk like that.

Poised there, in the middle of the city, before the seat of troubled democracy, looking across the bridge at the immense stone stretch of the Place de la Concorde, you can go in a dozen different, inviting directions. Because it is lunchtime, there is not much traffic, since all Paris declares a profound truce with business between the hours of twelve and two. You would not be surprised if you heard that the underworld had an unwritten agreement with the police not to pick a pocket or knife an associate at lunchtime.

Back across the bridge there is the restaurant in which each year the jury meets and has lunch while they vote the Prix Goncourt to the best novel of the year by a young writer. After reading about the Prize lunch in the papers, you can go to the restaurant the day following such a meeting on the intelligent assumption that any place good enough for ten middle-aged, successful French writers deserved your patronage.

Or you can wander down along the riverside, past the Beaux-Arts, which has been responsible for so much fine painting, since almost every good French artist has studied there at one time or another and has left swearing to violate every principle he was taught within its walls. And sticking to the river, you can go to the restaurant on the corner of the Place Saint-Michel and sit at a window on the second floor and look across at Notre Dame while you eat wild duck with blood sauce, or you can go to the restaurant on the Quai de la Tournelle that is decorated with large jars of pickles and photographs of wrestlers being hurled through the air. On the way, you can look at the paintings in the windows or fuss around the bookstalls and pick up magazines that were printed under the Germans during the Occupation and that are ostensibly banned, or buy an ornately printed card that contains an invocation to Paris by Victor Hugo and that reads in part:

Cities are bibles of stone. This city possesses no single dome, roof or pavement which does not convey some message of alliance and of union, and which does not offer some lesson, example or advice. Let the people of all the world come to this prodigious alphabet of monuments, of tombs and of trophies to learn peace and to unlearn the meaning of hatred. Let them be confident. For Paris has proven itself. To have once been Lutèce and to have become Paris—what could be a more magnificent symbol! To have been mud and to have become spirit!

At lunch you can remember that Victor Hugo also said, "Paris is the ceiling of the human race," after which he was forced to flee to the islands of Jersey and Guernsey, where he remained for the eighteen years of Napoleon III's reign. When he returned they began naming streets and squares after him and they have scarcely stopped since. Parisians seem to have a habit of exiling their heroes, or guillotining them, and making up for it later with street markers. Voltaire prudently spent a good deal of his life in Germany and Switzerland, and when in due course they came to bury him in the Panthéon they discovered that his heart was missing, and the rumor is that it was mislaid in a desk drawer that was sold by a junkman. Danton paid with his head for his activities in the city, but the city replaced it with the bronze statue of him on the Place de l'Odéon. Poor Courbet, too, who painted women's breasts so well, took down the statue of Napoleon from its pedestal on the Vendôme Column during the Commune on the grounds that it was a warlike and inartistic creation. Then, when the tide of government changed, he was put in jail and had to turn into a painter of fruits and vegetables because they wouldn't allow his models into the jail. And much later, the government demanded that he pay the costs of restoring the monument, which came to 323,000 francs. His paintings were seized as partial payment, and with the balance staring him in the face he fled to Switzerland, where he died, and now, of course, there is a Passage Courbet in Passy.

Replete with lunch and praising the wine and happy that you will be hungry again in six hours, you and your girl leave the restaurant and find the Rue de Seine, where the little art galleries, the antique shops, and the butcher shops stand side by side. There are larks in boxes on the butchers' marble tables, and partridge and wild doves flutter dead and head down, their wings outspread, in long strings across the open fronts of the stores, and the butchers in their sweaters and aprons look ruddy and frozen and keep blowing on their hands all winter. You buy a snuffbox and price some silver and haggle over a candlestick and notice the influence of Picasso on everybody and go into a tiny gallery that is having a *vernissage* of the works of a young painter who makes a specialty of lonely, moonlit cold walls around abandoned, dreamlike ports. The little room is crowded with people who are not looking at the pictures. There is a great deal of conversation and the young painter is standing alone in a corner, looking lonely and moonlit and abandoned.

You walk toward the Rodin Museum, which is not too

far away, because you want to show your girl the thirty-nine statues of Balzac that the sculptor produced out of his relentless energy and inspired dissatisfaction when he was commissioned to create a monument of the novelist to be erected at the intersection of the boulevards Raspail and Montparnasse. On the way you pass a horsemeat shop, under its sign of a gilded equine head, and you peer into a pharmacy window and see a celluloid contraption, equipped with a movable disk, with lines and dates and numbers drawn on it and advertised as a fecundity meter in this country which frowns on more direct methods of birth control.

There is also a rolling pin with rubber spikes that is guaranteed to work off excess fat, and a preparation for the skin that is supposed to ward off old age. The prescription desk is usually busy, because French doctors rarely carry medicines with them, and if they are to inject you with anything, they send you to the nearest drugstore to buy it yourself before their next visit.

There is a dressmaker's shop that advertises mourning outfits in twelve hours, convenient to an undertaker's that has photographs in its window of some of its better funerals, and a furniture shop that offers Provençal and bourgeois furniture and an electrical-appliance shop that offers for sale a refrigerator which makes only enough ice every forty-eight hours for one long glass of lemonade.

There are placards and posters and signs on all the walls. The Communists are calling a meeting to denounce American activities in Korea, Italy, and Greece, and the anti-Communists have made a list of all the leaders of the Russian Revolution, politicians, artists, writers, and scientists, who have been purged since 1917. There is a small, neat sign advertising the address of a gentleman who deals professionally in occultism, palm reading, cards, horoscopes, and the return of affection. His hours are from ten to five, except on Sundays, and by appointment. At the bottom of the advertisement he guarantees serious work.

Wood and coal can be ordered at the counters of many of the bars, and you can bet on the horses in the bars that advertise that they represent the Pari-Mutuel Urbain. Tickets for the national lottery are also being sold from little gaily-decorated stands, and you buy a chance and hope you are going to win five hundred thousand francs. You have bought a ticket every week, but you have not yet won five hundred thousand francs.

Many of the older women you pass are in black, giving the street a village air, and you notice a new provocative style of black jeans and tennis shoes for the young girls who live in the Latin Quarter, studying art or posing for artists or just living in the Quarter. There is a bar nearby where they serve Martinique rum punch almost exclusively, hot or cold, syrupy and deathly sweet, but the bar is always crowded just the same with people who are planning a magazine or criticizing a writer or wiring home for money.

The Rodin Museum, close to the martial austerities of the Invalides and the Ecole de Guerre, is in two buildings—the old Hôtel Byron and the chapel, which at one time was consecrated to the devotions of the nuns of the Sacred Heart. The nuns were dispossessed in one of the surges of anticlericalism that have left their mark on French history, and Rodin bought the property and moved his blocks of stone into the vaulted, high, lead-windowed chapel; and even now, after so many years of being at home there, the oversized, passionate, bare

figures seem strange in their invincibly religious surroundings.

You go out of the gallery into the garden, where,
among the thirty-nine studies, stands your favorite statue
of a man of letters: Balzac, in bronze, glaring at the Paris
he memorialized as a jungle of rapacity, betrayal, greed,
ambition, and intrigue, to the applause of generations of
Parisians. He stands there, fat, big-bellied, powerful,
mustached, aging, defiant, forbidding, with a hint of
almost-madness in his metal eyes, and he stands there
naked. It is as though the sculptor had said to himself,
Well, you have told everything about us, you deserve to
have everything told about you.

Your girl blinks, because she is not used to such
complete tributes to literature, and you speculate on what
would happen in America if the custom spread there and
some devout society established a similar statue of Mark
Twain in Hannibal, Missouri, or a full-length bronze,
sans fig leaf, of Emerson, in Concord, Massachusetts.

You drift away from Rodin and hail a taxi in front
of the bronze cannons of Napoleon's wars and the two
tanks of our own war that stand in front of the Invalides.
Geared for the moment to museums, you say, ''The
Louvre,'' to the driver and he starts frantically toward the
Right Bank. The taxi was built in the 1930's and smells
of twenty-year-old leather and the perfume of the lady
who has just been delivered to a great mansion nearby in
Proust's territory, the Faubourg Saint-Germain. The
driver hurls himself into traffic like a small boy jumping
into a haystack from the second story of a barn and
snarls insults at other drivers of an obscenity that would
start a blood feud in Tennessee.

The traffic policemen you pass on corners wave impatiently for you to go faster, and you shudder as you swerve down on bicyclists, pedestrians, and ladies with baby carriages. Motorcyclists pass you, with their wives riding behind them, both of them wearing padded helmets, as though before starting out they always assumed, with debonair pessimism, that they would be thrown on their heads at least once on each trip. Neatly dressed business gentlemen putt-putt alongside on small Vespas, with briefcases between their legs and miniature plastic windshields strapped to their foreheads.

There is a cynical joke drivers repeat about the law of the road in Paris: "To hit a pedestrian in the street—that is sport. But to hit him in the *clous*—that is sadism." The *clous* is the crossing between curbs that is marked by iron buttons for the use of people on foot, and you have a feeling that thousands of Parisians have met their end in these deceptive sanctuaries. Somewhere you have heard a dark apocryphal statistic—that one driver out of every twelve in Paris has killed his man. On foot, the Parisian is as courteous as the citizen of any other city. But mounted, he is merciless. Memories of the Bourbon era, when the coaches of nobles clattered heedlessly through the narrow streets, crushing pedestrians unlucky enough to be in their path, must seethe through a Parisian's brain as soon as he has a wheel in his hands.

Charging across the Pont Alexandre III, the driver grumbles about the usual natural enemies of taxi drivers anywhere—the police. The police, it seems, have proposed that all taxi drivers take a physical examination every five years to determine their fitness to continue in their profession. "For me," the driver said, "it is nothing. I am a young man of fifty. But what of the drivers who are eighty years old, who started driving hansom cabs sixty years ago and know nothing else? They have no livers left, no eyes, no kidneys. How can they be expected to pass a physical examination? It is inhuman.''

There is nothing you can do but agree—and hope, silently, that whatever eighty-year-old taxi pilots ply their trade in Paris are partial to neighborhoods you rarely visit.

In the museum you are firm in forbidding a general tour, from which you would only come out stunned, foot-worn, adrift in the looted centuries. You go dutifully to the ''Mona Lisa,'' behind its glass and its little velvet rope, because your girl wants to see her, but you have seen so many prints and read about the picture so often that the smile is just a faint, fogged glimmer behind its mist of associations.

You leave the great paintings for another day, because they transcend Paris, transcend France, and you stand in front of the enormous battle pieces of Delacroix, which find an echo in the voices of all the French generals who still keep saying today, ''Glory!'' and ''Attack!'' As you look at the brightly colored tunics, the pretty smoke, the rearing horses, the clean, unreal dying, you regret the disappearance of the sword and the horse from the battlefield, the discovery of neutral khaki and field gray, and the ubiquitous presence of photographers at our own wars.

You leave the Louvre and pass Joan of Arc, gold on her gilt horse, and enter your favorite museum in all the world, the Musée du Jeu de Paume, where the great Impressionists have been collected and where, even on the grayest winter afternoon, sunshine seems to be pouring from the walls. Here Cézanne and Renoir and Monet and Manet and Degas and Pissarro announce that air is good to breathe, that women are delightful to look at, that food is good to eat, that wine is good to drink, that the world, be it a Paris street or a garden in Chatou or a village in the Midi, is worthy to be lived in. In this small, clean building, with the roar of traffic coming in through the windows from the crowded Place de la Concorde outside, you find a robust and delicious corrective to our times and a powerful antidote to suicide.

Many of the pictures are superb, but there are two that you could look at forever. There is the huge, mischievous "Déjeuner sur l'Herbe" by Manet, with the comfortable, bearded gentlemen seated at their ease beneath the trees and the picnic lunch, and the long, magnificent nude girl, staring gravely out at you in troubling contrast to her fully dressed gentlemen friends. The girl seems to be saying, "Do you see anything wrong? *I* don't." And over the entire thing there hangs a mocking air of repletion, health, and rakish innocence that makes whatever picnics you have had in your own life seem, in retrospect, discouragingly incomplete.

The other picture is by Degas, and it is simply of two laundresses, ironing. They are both young women with careless hair and round, solid arms, and one of them is stretching and yawning, but there is a pink, golden, late-afternoon light on them and a sense of the cheerful celebration of the homely, holy, sensual everyday, and when you go out once more into the street the people of the second half of the twentieth century who throng past seem inexcusably wan and dun-colored.

You pause at the corner and look down at the Church of the Madeleine and congratulate yourself for being in a city where a copy of the Parthenon stands, surrounded by flower stalls and delicatessens. You go to Hédiard, the most famous of the delicatessens, which has been at the same spot since 1851 and which smells peppery and fragrant, and you order a basket of kumquats and a kilo of sweet potatoes, which are a rarity in Paris, and an avocado, which is seldom seen in the markets, and a jar of black English marmalade and a small, dry, spiced sausage and a great jar of sweet stewed raspberries and some preserved ginger root and a pound of lichee nuts.

You walk up the Rue du Faubourg-Saint-Honoré, which is a dangerous thing to do with a girl on any day but Sunday, when the shops are closed, because here are the most expensive windows in the world. You admire a polished side saddle and a pair of silvery spurs and a suede jacket and a silk scarf printed with the flags of the ancient baronies and fine lisle socks with clocks more brilliant than any you would dare wear, and you pass the British Embassy, where the guards, with the red bands around their caps, stand at attention, looking overdisciplined and British.

You tell your girl that if she is very rich she will dress more handsomely here in Paris than anywhere else in the world, but otherwise will do better at any department store in the United States, because in France there is none of the mass production of pretty clothes that is Seventh Avenue's gift to America and that has made American women of all classes so generally pleasing to the eye. But you promise to look for someone who knows someone else who has her dresses made by a copyist to whom the mannequins of several important houses smuggle out models overnight and who, with blithe immorality, will make you a reasonable facsimile for less than a third the price of the original.

You also tell your girl to beware of French shoes, because all the American women you know are constantly complaining that French feet are different from American feet and you have seen the look of pain produced on the face of an American lady who had been to a Parisian bootmaker when it was suggested that she walk three blocks to a theater.

You think of going to the Museum of Modern Art, on the hill of Chaillot, where there is an exhibition of Mexican art—which is a kind of point-by-point denial of every brush stroke you have seen in the Jeu de Paume. There everything is oversize, distorted, tragic, violent, rebellious; there a monstrous painted figure with a head that is not human but that looks as though it had been made of flesh which has turned to stone, stretches out two grotesque hands in agony, supplication, and threat.

To maintain emotional balance you take your girl to a couturier's, which is having a final rehearsal of its new show before the grand opening the next day. You are early and you seat yourself in the newly painted oblong room with the narrow, raised platform running down the middle, as the room fills with the heads of the various departments, women in charge of the buying of material, the women in charge of the hats, the women in charge of furs, the *vendeuses*. Around the entrance stand the seamstresses, modest and birdlike, to watch their glorious sisters parade in their finery.

The owner-designer comes out and everybody stands up for him like war correspondents honoring a three-star general in a press conference. He makes a graceful little speech, praising his co-workers for their loyalty in the past and assuring himself of their loyalty in the future. He tells them all to notice the elliptical motif of the skirts this season and reminds them that what was called raw silk last year will be called *soie sauvage*, ''wild silk,'' during this. There is a little nervous hush while everybody prays that the designer, from whose quick hands come all their livelihoods, will not have lost his touch this time.

All through the fashionable district, where the grand couturiers have their mansions—on the Avenue Montaigne, on the Avenue George V, on the Place Vendôme, in all the busy, nerve-racked establishments where Paris erects, twice each year, its most glittering monument to frivolity—the same scene is being enacted during this week.

The first girl comes out, swinging slowly along the ramp in that arrogant walk that has cost so many men so much money, and the show is on, interrupted from time to time by bursts of applause for a particular dress.

One pretty dark girl is never applauded, although as far as you can tell, her dresses are on a level with the others. ''She doesn't *sell* the dresses any more,'' the woman next to you whispers. ''Last year they applauded her all the time. But she's engaged to be married now, her fiancé gave her a ring big enough to choke a horse, and she isn't interested any more.''

A girl comes out in a plain blue suit, and the woman next to you says, ''That will sell to all the bourgeoisie. It's a bourgeois suit and we put it on the girl with a bourgeois face.''

For a moment you're glad you're not a girl, glad you're not French, and glad you're not modeling clothes in the abattoir-efficient atmosphere of a great fashion house.

A plumpish girl comes out in a flashy pencil-striped white suit, and the woman next to you says, ''That's for the Spaniards.''

''Don't forget the South Americans,'' says the woman sitting next to her.

''And the Portuguese,'' says a lady across the room.

There are seven girls to show one hundred and ten dresses in one hour and a half, and there are scenes of frantic zippering and buttoning behind the dressing-room door, but there is no delay, and each girl comes sauntering out radiant, perfectly accoutered, and not breathing hard, a living rebuke to all wives who keep their husbands waiting the last bitter half-hour while they get themselves up for the evening.

The last dress you see before you have to leave is a ''court dress.'' It is white, with glass pendants in glittering diagonal lines on the skirt and bosom. The girl who wears it is tall and blond and has a tiara in her hair and a choker of pearls around her throat, and in her regal, extravagant, top-heavy, and slightly ludicrous dress, she shines as princesses should, yet rarely do, and you hope she is not living in a single disordered room on the Left Bank with a drunken photographer who takes her money and makes passes at all her friends.

Now you have to go to a cocktail party. It is a kind of housewarming, being given by a friend who waited for fifteen years to get this apartment, whose occupant has conveniently died. His old apartment, which was one floor above, had only three rooms, and this one has four.

He really needs five rooms. On the floor below there is a five-room apartment. He inquires politely about the health of the tenant and looks forward patiently to the next fifteen years.

At the cocktail party there is gin, expensively imported from England, which shows that the host is serious about this collection of guests. People are standing in groups, smoking French cigarettes, which make your mouth smell like a small industrial town after you have gone through half a pack. Three or four of the guests have rosettes of the Legion of Honor, and a plump, intelligent-looking lawyer is defending the ancient practice of dueling.

"There are arguments," he says, "that cannot be taken to law and that can only be settled by the duel. Otherwise they go on and on forever, with people cutting each other at dinners and in offices and making everybody uncomfortable and bored. A duel has the quality of a period at the end of a paragraph, and civilized life has need of such periods."

In a corner, a group of Frenchmen are talking. "Americans," one of them says, "Americans may think they come to Paris for a number of reasons: to be artists, to be restless, to be young, to be free . . . but essentially they are all here in the same capacity. As archaeologists. To study antiquity. Nobody comes to the Paris of today, because Paris is a city of the past. Everybody visits a Paris that no longer exists except in ruins and memory."

"Paris is the only real city," adds another. "New York is four villages, London an industry, Rio de Janeiro a place where you have the feeling you must behave as though you are a schoolboy in a religious institution. Everything is possible in Paris, everything can be said, everybody can be met, often on the same day. It is the one city in the world that is not provincial."

And a sixty-year-old painter, looking back on his career and all the invitations he had accepted, says, "In Paris, fame is a telephone call."

Another guest has just come from a cocktail party that is a monthly feature given by a great publishing house for all its authors. "You could tell whose books weren't selling this season," the guest says. "They brought their wives and they never moved away from the hors d'oeuvre table."

"Let me explain about our government," a little round man with enormous glasses is saying to an American lady. "It is always falling and it is always Radical Socialist."

"There is only one country in the world," a journalist is saying, "that is rich enough to permit capitalism to work—and that is America. In France, capitalism cannot work." He pauses for a moment, reflecting on what he has said, then smiles happily. "In fact," he adds, "in France socialism cannot work. In fact, in France nothing can work."

A handsome white-haired politician, who is being baited by some young intellectuals, turns brick red and moves to the attack. "Why don't you just drink Coca-Cola and get it over with?" he demands. "All you young people are secretly Americans at heart. All you want is security."

The editor of a publishing house is introduced to a successful writer. The editor bows and says, "When you feel yourself on the verge of committing an infidelity to your publisher, I trust you will come and visit me."

A smartly dressed woman of a certain age is standing in a corner with her arm affectionately around the shoulders of a well-known young author. "Darling," she is saying, "why don't you write the way you really are? Rosy and funny and healthy. Why are you always writing those long sad books, full of the *saloperies* of youth, with all the people going to bed with everybody else?"

You leave because you want to go to the theater and there is just time for dinner before the curtain.

You go to the restaurant opposite the Odéon, where you can sit on the glassed-in terrace and look across the little square to the Greek-styled theater, now taken over by the Comédie Française and whose columns are illuminated each night by marvelously theatrical blue floodlights. Just after the Liberation you could meet Jean Cocteau at that restaurant, and Christian Bérard, bearded and carrying a tawny, long-furred cat. You could also get a fluffy chocolate mousse there, made with American Army chocolate whose availability was no doubt connected with the nightly presence of the smiling, well-fed American soldier at the bar who must have been a mess sergeant.

Now it is crowded and fashionable and there is a rich smell of bouillabaisse in the air and you can eat your favorite oysters there, the enormous, deep-sea-tasting *fines de claires,* which are scorned by the epicures who favor the subtler Belons and Marennes and who call the *claire,* or *Portugaise,* the workingman's oyster. The sommelier, who has an almost incomprehensible Midi accent, carries a corkscrew with an obscene device on it, but the wines are good and it is pleasant to sit there looking across at the floodlit columns and watching the polite people arriving for *Cyrano.*

If *Cyrano* doesn't tempt you, you can see *Antigone*

tonight or a dozen plays whose central theme is that of the cuckolded husband, including one in which the cuckolded husband is the magistrate who condemns to death for murder the man who was cozily tucked away in a hotel with the magistrate's wife on the afternoon on which the crime was committed. This last play, not unnaturally, drew some pained letters from the company of magistrates, who are overworked and underpaid and who feel sorry enough for themselves as it is.

You can even see a play that was put on at a little art theater and became a great success largely because it was a comedy that was not about cuckolded husbands.

You can see Molière or Racine or Bernstein or Sartre or Anouilh, the last a kind of one-man trust who pours out a seemingly inexhaustible stream of bitter, witty, elegant, slightly constructed popular plays that follow so quickly on the heels of one another that there is a jealous legend about him that he writes all day every day, and whenever he reaches twenty thousand words, sends them down to the nearest theater to be produced immediately.

The acting is generally of a high quality and gives evidence of solid, protracted training. The productions vary enormously, ranging from plays that are brilliantly mounted and directed to a makeshift level of scenic improvisation far below the standard of the most mediocre Broadway offering.

In the theater, at even the gravest plays, you are likely to be distracted between acts by magic-lantern slides advertising silk stockings, raincoats, shampoos, and studios that make a specialty of photographing infants.

There is a movement afoot to attract the tourist trade by installing earphones into which will be poured a running English translation of the script as it is being played. Some of the language of the Paris stage, which is remarkably free, may have explosive effects on unaccustomed American ears when it is put into plain Anglo-Saxon English.

It is midnight by the time you get out of the theater. In Saint-Germain the ugliest bars in the world are jammed with the young unwashed of half a dozen countries, and a lanky recent graduate of Yale is announcing to the crowded sidewalk tables that his girl is deceiving him inside with the second son of an Indian prince. Nobody sympathizes with him and he laughs, showing the good old Yale spirit, and sits down and has a glass of beer.

On the Champs Elysées the girls are prowling like jaguars, twitching their fur neckpieces under the cold, controlled stares of the police. The movies are letting out and everybody has been to see *An American in Paris* and the couples are kissing frankly in the side streets. A young man, slightly drunk, comes up to an American group and bows and says, "You are Americans. Naturally, you are not Communists. You do not have to work at the lathe. I, however, have to work at the lathe, so you must forgive me if I would do everything in my power to force you to the lathe." He says, "Thank you," and wanders politically and incoherently off in the direction of Passy.

In the nightclubs sad girls are singing that they hate Sunday, and there is a dancing horse and young men who sing that the Seine flows and flows and flows and sings and sings and sings and is a mistress in whose bed Paris sleeps. Off the Place Pigalle dark figures whisper out of the shadows, asking if you want to see a show, and in the big cafés, devoted to the almost-nude female body, parade all shapes of girls, bare from the waist up but conforming to police regulations below that. After their turn, the girls line up, demure in ball gowns, on the staircase, and you can dance with them, if you will, by buying a ticket. Like most Frenchwomen, they dance so tightly clasped to you that you feel like an infant strangling in his crib under blankets that have been tucked in too well.

In a Russian nightclub, where all the talent is over fifty years old, they play guitars and dance gypsy dances and sit around candles in a group and sing sorrowful winter songs and come to your table and drink to your health with your own champagne, after which you have to drain your glass and break it on the table in honor of the Czar, or in honor of yourself, or in honor of the price of the champagne.

Needing air, you and your girl walk to the river and step onto a tiny, crowded floating bar that is attached to a launch, and with a glass in your hand and feeling, No, this is too romantic, chug off up the black river toward the cathedral. The city is quiet on both sides of you, the river wind is cool, the trees on the banks are fitfully illuminated by the headlights of occasional automobiles crossing the bridges. The bums are sleeping on the *quais,* waiting to be photographed at dawn by the people who keep turning out the glossy picture books on Paris; a train passes somewhere nearby, blowing its whistle, which sounds like a maiden lady who has been pinched, surprisingly, by a deacon; the buildings of the politicians and the diplomats are dark; the monuments doze; the starlit centuries surround you on the dark water. . . .

You turn, hesitantly, toward the girl at your side. . . .

You blink. It is daylight and you are still at the same café table. Your girl has never arrived, of course. At the table next to you a woman is saying, "I have a friend on *Le Figaro*. He says the war will start in September. What do you think will happen in Paris?"

"Paris," says the man who is sitting with her, "Paris will be spared."

"Why?"

"Because Paris is always spared," the man says and orders a coffee.

Searle's Paris: II

Variations

$\mathcal{S}$O . . . that was the way it was—or seemed to be—to one rather bemused observer long ago. To many of us who lived in the place, that time is recalled as the good old days.

The uniforms of the United States Army, Navy, and Air Force, with all the old familiar campaign ribbons, were everywhere to be seen, and NATO, with its famed American commanders, was a comforting presence in the city, and France was a gallant and reliable ally, at least in the public prints, and the PX in the American Embassy dispensed New World bounty like maple syrup and refrigerators and duty-free bourbon to the deserving troops and diplomats and their deserving friends.

Charles de Gaulle was an aging, rusticated general, writing his memoirs in lapidary prose in a tiny, forgotten village called Colombey-les-Deux-Eglises that one passed through in two minutes on the way to skiing in Switzerland. Somehow the sun never seemed to be shining over its humble old roofs as the car sped past the town. Whatever happened to France, everybody said, would happen without General de Gaulle.

It was true that in our native land Senator McCarthy was savaging civilization, and John Foster Dulles and the Russians were planning God knows what horrors for us in the future, but for a while we were out of our own mainstream and only bracingly touched by the currents of Europe. Selfishly, we made the most of our luck. We had had our war, and Paris for that period was part of our reward, although in our bones we knew that what we had could not last, that vistas would change, work fail, girls marry, friends fall away, places of pleasure close their doors, old songs lose their magic, weather change.

* * *

People are always writing about cities to be happy in. Let me be contrary for a moment. Let me write for those who are unhappy and are looking for a city to be unhappy in. Let me write about Paris in the winter.

Paris in the winter is for connoisseurs of melancholy —lovers soon to be parted, merchants on the edge of bankruptcy, poets caught between rhymes and remittance men caught between checks, horse owners whose steeds have just come in last, playwrights who have just had a failure, women whose husbands have left them for younger, prettier, smarter, richer, and all-round *better* girls; Paris in the winter is for deposed kings, discovered spies, leaders of peace movements; for people who owe money to the government—any government; for the editors of little magazines who don't dare go to their office because the printer is waiting there with the bill; for children who don't dare to go home because they have just been given their report cards; Paris in the winter is for brave men who have fought in the wars of this century and who have just read the morning newspaper; for tipplers struggling with the drink; for pregnant unwed girls; for the gentlemen friends of pregnant unwed girls; for movie stars on the way down and movie stars on the way up; for people who get their names in the papers too often and for people who don't get them in often enough; for widows whose husbands have left most of the estate to charity, for disinherited sons, for gamblers who have used up their luck.

Weeks on end the sun is only a pale rumor beyond the slowly moving clouds, and the soft gray sky above the rooftops seems to be about to break into a low, musical sobbing, ready to commiserate with criminals in flight from the police, with middleweights who have been knocked out in the first round. On December afternoons the city extends its stone sympathy to grounded pilots, to sufferers from jealousy, either well- or ill-founded, to newspapermen who have been switched to the night shift, to policemen with sore feet and sopranos with a cough and airplane salesmen who have not sold a jet fighter to Germany in two years. Antique dealers stuck with Louis Quinze commodes that were manufactured at the time of Léon Blum find a reciprocal sorrow in the drizzling streets, and the art collector who has just realized his prize Renoir is a fake discovers the climate of the Seine basin was made for his mood.

Here and there an Englishman can be found happy on brandy in a crowded restaurant, but after London in the wintertime, it is difficult to be unhappy anywhere. And to balance the unchilled Anglo-Saxon there will be the Greek waiter looking out through the misted restaurant window, haunted by the memory of Aegean sunlight, and a native of Mississippi writing his first novel, his imagination inflamed but his blood thinned by his heritage, hunched before a derisively tepid radiator in a hotel off the Place de l'Odéon that should have been condemned at the time of General Boulanger.

Paris in the winter is made to be a background for small disasters and piercing personal disappointments, for the hostess who is called to the telephone at eight-fifteen at night to be told that the dinner for forty people that she is giving that evening will have to do without the guest of honor because he has the grippe or has been arrested. It is the season and the place for mothers whose marriageable daughters have been staying out all night for six months with counts who turn out to have descended from a family of plumbers in Sicily; for American emissaries who come to France with the idea of persuading President de Gaulle to do something he doesn't want to do, or to do anything at all; for representatives of American firms who arrive in Paris for the first time believing everything they have been told back in Chicago about French women; for American women who arrive in Paris for the first time believing everything they have been told back in St. Louis about French men; for tennis players who have just turned pro and believe they can beat Gonzales when they get him on the courts of the Stade Coubertin; for retired generals who have just read what other retired generals have written about them in their memoirs.

Paris in the wintertime is the city for misogynists, misanthropes, and pessimists, for students of history who believe that the whole thing is all one long downhill ride; for all lovers of the human race who are ready to shake their heads at man's ingratitude, to deplore the world's slack forgetfulness, and to weigh the vanity of mortal achievements. Paris is a city studded with monuments, and its streets are named in honor of departed great men, but who knows what General Rochambeau did at the battle of Yorktown that entitles him to wear a bronze sword in front of the Fiat Garage on the Rue de Chaillot; who hums a tune of Ambroise Thomas's as he tries to find a place to park on the street that bears the composer's name; who looks up into the damp sky and sees noble wings and hears the throb of brave primitive engines when he ducks into an espresso bar out of the rain on the Rue Jean Mermoz? Who is cured of anything today on the Rue Dr. V. Hutinel? Does anyone recite *"Sur le*

printemps de ma jeunesse folle, je ressemblais à l'hiron-
delle qui vole, puis ça, puis là . . ." as he gets his hair cut
on the Rue Clément Marot? Where are the descendants
of Pierre Premier de Serbie? Where is Serbia? Who,
going into the Museum of Modern Art on the Avenue du
Président Wilson, can honestly say he has lived up to
the President's Fourteen Points? These are the January
thoughts of Paris.

Paris is constantly being compared to a beautiful
woman, and if the comparison is just, in the wintertime
Paris is a beautiful woman who has come back two weeks
before from a holiday in the sun and who has lost her tan
and is now in that unhealthy yellow state that makes the
aftermath of vacations look like the onset of jaundice. If
Paris is beautiful and feminine in the spring and summer,
when the city's two hundred and ninety-five thousand
trees put out their leaves, it is the beauty of a fine-boned
old lady, with a bright green scarf cunningly thrown
around her, making you forget the wrinkles. Winter lays
the bones of the city bare, and the old lady shows her age.

Paris in the winter is for sad geographers, for the
makers of mournful maps, for tourists with a taste for
visiting places from which joy has fled. For such amateurs
of sorrow, let me offer the Assemblée Nationale, stuffed
with politicians to whom nobody listens and who propose
laws that nobody obeys. Pass into the dark red hall, with
its rows of banked benches, and hear the echo of speeches
that were once made there—hear Gambetta's voice, listen
for the lost powerful intonations of Clemenceau and

Herriot, and think a long hard thought about democracy. For winter traveling go to La Santé. This is the prison near Montparnasse, a region that has long been known for its mingled hilarity and culture but that allows little of its tingling qualities to reach as far as the prison walls just off its boundaries. Look at the grim pile and think of the crime accumulated there, the murder, arson, extortion, embezzlement, the breaking and entering, the sedition, pimping, the offense against public morals, the theft with violence, the debauchery of the young, the cruelty to children, the bomb-placing and acid-throwing, the horse-doping and the sale of drugs to minors, the adulteration of foods and counterfeiting of old masters, the smuggling and perjury and incitement to desertion, the intelligence with the enemy and the nonassistance to persons in danger. There are many persons in danger in the winter in Paris, and the nonassistance assumes monumental proportions. Walk back along the boulevard away from the prison, where tomorrow morning they may be guillotining the son of a good family who poured gasoline over a girl and set her afire near Fontainebleau because she no longer wished to share her earnings as a prostitute with him, walk back toward the gaudy signs of the striptease *salons* a few blocks away and reflect on how many dire purposes one neighborhood in a modern city can serve.

To grieve about better times, stroll through the Bois de Boulogne in early February, when winter seems to have lasted all your life, and see the riders emerging from the mist, the hoofs of their mounts throwing up mud as they canter past the lake on which in summer young men strum guitars while their girls row them among the swans. In February think of all the dead roses of the Bagatelle, think of the girls who danced under the trees at the great balls Ali Khan used to give on the night of the Grand Prix at the Pré Catelan, now shuttered against the wind and looking as if it had heard its last music, served its last pitcherful of champagne tinted with crushed wild strawberries. Still in the Bois, search out, with displeasure, the newly erected hall where electrified bowling alleys resound to the rumble of strikes and spares, and reflect upon the incursion of neon and mechanized amusement into the natural world. See the foresters raking up dead leaves and cutting down wide-spreading sycamores and chestnuts that look as though they could stand three hundred years but that are really rotten at the core, dead from breathing the air of Paris.

Walk out of the Bois along the Avenue du Général Koenig and look at the houseboats tied to the banks of the river, their summer paint flaked, their cold hulls streaming with dank strands of weeds, among eddies of orange peels. Think of the suicides fished up below the nearest bridge and note the choked warrens of jerrybuilt apartment houses that cover the ridge on the other side of the river where not long ago there were tennis courts and gardens.

Station yourself at the gate of an *école communale* and observe how pale and greenish are the children as they emerge into the winter dankness, how much in need of handkerchiefs they all are, how prematurely aged. Remember how they have passed the long day, not permitted to drink water when they were thirsty or to go to the bathroom when they were bored. Talk to them and be shocked at how educated and sophisticated they are, and find out that they have been taught the one dreadful Parisian lesson—compete or perish.

Watch their fathers and mothers as they drive through the Etoile and understand how well they, too, in their time, have learned the same lesson. Around the soaring monument of the Arc de Triomphe, with its carved statements of glory and aspiration, a race on wheels demonstrates just how much selfishness, egotism, impatience, bad manners, and carelessness of human life can be expressed with the aid of the internal combustion engine.

For weariness of heart and confirmation of the link between winter and the Industrial Revolution, come in on the commuters' trains to the Gare de l'Est from the suburbs of Chelles and Bobigny and Noisy-le-Sec. Stand with the gray-faced workingmen in the crowded trains as they pass their grim homes in the smoke-colored stone wound that is the northeastern edge of Paris. See with their eyes the tanned ladies in mink coming in on the next track from the season at Saint Moritz, and remember that the first commune was established in this city by the great-grandfathers of your fellow travelers, and how much blood was finally shed.

Do you agonize over religion? Go to a fashionable wedding, and while the bride approaches the altar on the arm of her father, listen to the conversation about the father from the lady dressed by Dior in the pew on your right.

Does litigation depress you? Do you sometimes feel that all the forests of the earth will eventually be felled to make paper for legal briefs? Do you have nightmares in which you are captive in a world where it will be necessary to consult a lawyer before putting your name on a visiting card, before giving birth to a child or having it christened, before speaking to a census taker or hiring a baby sitter, before burying your dog or buying an airplane ticket for Zurich? Go to the Palais de Justice and count the lawyers whispering in the corridors, and try to forgive them for what they are whispering. Listen in at a hearing on a will that is being contested by members of the family of a deceased banker. Follow the arguments for a while and try to decide for yourself whether Papa was in full possession of his senses when he left the family's *maison particulière* on the Avenue Foch to the dancer at the Opéra who had been his great and good friend for the last ten years of his life. Or use your influence to get in to one of the big, splashy trials, one of the fat, scandalous ones that *tout Paris* follows more closely than the city's sporting element follows the Tour de France, and derive a dark satisfaction from realizing that everybody knows a great deal more than he is telling and that under a more reasonable system of jurisdiction almost everyone in the courtroom, probably including the bailiffs and one or two of the judges, would be clapped into jail. And to cap your despair, go across the river to the Faculté de Droit and see how many more lawyers there will be next year.

Slip into the nearest public hospital, past the maimed old charwomen knocked over by trucks as they tried to cross the streets in front of their houses, past the Algerians machine-gunned by mistake while they were having lunch, past the ladies wounded by husbands who arrived home unexpectedly—slip past them all, and if it is not Sunday or a holiday or dinnertime, you will be able to find a doctor and he will be able to tell you how many cases died of alcoholism that day in Paris. Go directly to the wine market, and in the odorous sheds try to buy your next year's supply of Burgundy, and be shocked at the price of last year's vintage.

Go to the Panthéon and ask yourself honestly if you would like to spend the winter underground in company with Mirabeau, Voltaire, Descartes, and J.-J. Rousseau.

March past the Ecole Militaire and glance, not too openly, at the generals and colonels going in and out, fingering their rosettes of the Legion of Honor, contemplating treason, sourly conscious of losing a great many wars.

Peer in at the art galleries where the new men, who paint in abstract bars and whorls and circles, seem finally, all to be shouting the same thing—"I am in pain." Think of Cézanne and Gauguin and Modigliani not selling any paintings in the city, and of Buffet selling too many.

Look at the theater posters. For winter solace there is Beckett and Ionesco and Anouilh and Genet, the one saying, "It is impossible to move," the other saying, "It is impossible to communicate," another saying, "It is impossible not to cheat and it is impossible not to be cheated."

Look at the open-air markets, where the housewives poke at the colorless vegetables of winter and say, "It is impossible to live on my husband's salary."

Look at the evening newspapers. No—on second thought, better not.

Wound yourself with nostalgia—hum the old songs and stroll along the *grands boulevards* where the billboards outside the movie houses are adorned with half-naked purplish young starlets forty feet tall and various young actors with guns in their hands. The *brasseries* are pitilessly lit and look dirty and the waiters overworked and undertipped and the customers, wrapped in mufflers and overcoats, sit on the glassed *terrasses* under the infrared heaters in a stubborn parody of summer. Everything is honky-tonk and designed to make you want to go right home and weed out the old songs from your record collection. The new songs blare out tinnily from the doorways of phonograph shops, making you feel that nobody knows how to write a song or sing it any more. The girls are swathed in shapeless bulky coats, and in their martyrdom to nylon their legs are painfully blue from the cold as they hurry back to unrewarding jobs. They look forbidding and inaccessible, and the admirer of women sighs for another season when the same girls, dressed for sunny days and warm nights, seem to be the delightful property of every watcher in the city.

Glance idly at a map and follow the small wiggle of a street that certainly must have been christened in winter and whose name is a simple homesick cry of longing—the Rue du Cherche-Midi—which means, literally, the Street of the Search for the South. Recall how far north of the Mediterranean Paris lies and how many Mediterraneans are held within its walls. Ignore the fact that idiomatically a *cherche-midi* is translated as a sponger, a man who is looking for a free lunch. Try to forget that there was someone in a position of authority in the city who was sardonic enough to name a narrow little alley "Sponger Street."

In Paris in the winter you notice that there are fewer children on the streets and more ambulances, fewer women and more men, and always too many pigeons, being fed yesterday's bread by insane, antisocial old ladies who give no thought of the damage their feathered clients inflict on the statues of the capital or the millions of hours of sleep they cost the inhabitants of the city with their maddening early-morning cooing and gurgling and throbbing and burbling. If ever a city could use a race of mute and continent birds, it is Paris, and you are led to wonder, if trees and men die in breathing the air of the city, and if there is something in the atmosphere that keeps the human birth rate down, why it is that pigeons can thrive so noisily and propagate with such abandon?

Buildings collapse more frequently in Paris in the winter, jet planes fly lower, the helicopters churning the air above you on their way to and from Brussels and the motorbikes on the avenues flay your nerves with their inescapable mechanical coughing. At the *thés dansants* in the big halls, more of the couples turning gracelessly to the music are composed of girls who are waiting to be victimized by men and who you know will never be satisfied even in this modest ambition. In the evenings, in the restaurants, you are confronted everywhere with the picture of drab marital fidelity, long-married couples eating with their unsanitary dogs on the banquette between them, occasionally addressing a word to the beast and almost never to each other. What Parisians call *les vrais couples d'août* are hard to find. The true couples of August are usually composed of a man whose wife is at the seashore with the children and a pretty girl who is probably in Paris in August because she is modeling the autumn collections. The difference between ordinary winter couples and *les vrais couples d'août* is that the latter help bring a room alive because they have sought each other out, they are dining with each other voluntarily, they take pleasure in each other's company, and they have a great deal to say to each other.

You think of all the literary prizes that are bestowed in Paris, on the average of one a day, which makes about ninety a winter, and instead of sharing the satisfaction of merit rewarded felt by the winners, you ache with the heartburn of the ten thousand writers in the city who have won no prize that season and whose books are in the window of no bookstore that afternoon.

You wince at the cruelty of the city and remember the sentence spoken the night before about a lovely woman of thirty whose face used to be on the cover of all the magazines and who now cannot get a job posing for even the least ambitious of editors—"She's finished," the light voice said gaily, "she overdid it. You know how it is in this town. If they know your name they won't look at you."

In the winter you even feel sorry for news photographers, huddled, blowing on their frozen fingers, in their mass vigils outside the doors of the great hotels from which movie stars or visiting dignitaries may or may not emerge in time for the last edition. Later, when the newsmen are ordered to the Left Bank to cover a student riot, you are even sorrier for them as the police beat them over the head with clubs and break their expensive cameras, since policemen everywhere consider themselves kindly family men and are averse to having easily identified photographs published of themselves whacking young women across the back of the neck with lead-weighted capes.

Extend your sympathy to the owners of famous old restaurants, where nobody ever ate lunch in less than three hours, and who are now bowing to the times and transforming their dining rooms into snack bars. Stand at the sides of these defeated old apostles of joy as they watch their wine cellars being auctioned off, as the Burgundy goes in gross lots, as the names of the great châteaux of the Gironde are called out, as the precious cases are carted away because it is improbable that anyone in the new chromium and plastic café will ever order a La Tâche 1929 with his ham sandwich or a Montrachet with his hamburger.

Think a sad thought for the ice-bound employees of the striptease joints, silent and glum as the Black Forest most of every evening and which only spring to life—the musicians tuning up, the girls adjusting their stockings— when a potential customer, a derelict from the preceding season's wave of tourists, pokes his head in and every-body smiles falsely and prepares to charge seventeen new francs (three dollars and forty cents) for a bottle of Alsatian beer.

Think of the old ladies in raveled sweaters congealed in the newspaper kiosks, of the salesgirls on their feet all day in the unheated grocery shops, of the oystermen open-ing a million shells a winter, their bare, swollen fingers laced in frozen seaweed on the windy streets; think of the demented young men prowling among the shuttered build-ings after midnight painting the Jeune Nation symbol on the walls of the city to let Parisians know fascism is not dead in France; think of the unbroken colts from the green fields of Ireland doomed to be slaughtered for meat tomorrow in the abattoir on the Boulevard Vaugirard.

The sad past presents its mingled claims, too, in the winter in Paris, and the mind is assailed by dark mem-ories: of Napoleon, retired on half-pay at the age of twenty, with the rank of lieutenant, eating frugally to save sous and worried that all the wars were over; of Ney, whom Napoleon called the bravest of the brave, offering to bring his ex-commander back to the Bourbon king in a cage when Napoleon was on his way up from Elba; of Balzac hiding from his creditors on the Rue Raynouard; of the Duc d'Enghien being treacherously brought before a firing squad at three o'clock in the morning a hundred and fifty years ago in the moat at the Château de Vincennes; of Edith Piaf singing "La Vie en Rose" just after the war, and *"La fille de joie est triste, au coin d'la rue, là-bas. Son accordéoniste, il est parti soldat . . ."* You see Maurice Chevalier at an opening night and notice that he is growing old and losing his voice, you see Georges Carpentier, white-haired and impeccable as a foreign minister, in the front rows on Monday nights for the bouts at the Palais des Sports, and you remember when he was the *chevalier sans peur and sans reproche,* with a big right hand but not heavy enough for his job when he was knocked out by Jack Dempsey in the fourth round at Boyle's Thirty Acres on the Jersey flats outside Newark, with nobody around him speaking enough French to help much as he went down for the last time. You remember Hitler at the Arc de Triomphe and Goering at Maxim's and the Louvre; you remember F. Scott Fitzgerald drunk at the Ritz bar, writing his best book and getting his worst reviews. You thumb through the new anti-novels in the bookshops and wonder what it must have been like to be Guy de Maupassant on the way to Dr. Blanche's asylum, what Dumas must have been thinking of when, old and passé, he allowed himself to be photographed with Adah Mencken sitting on his lap. You try to understand how great a weight of suffering a man must have borne to write, as Verlaine wrote, *"Il pleure dans mon coeur comme il pleut sur la ville."*

Winter, like unhappiness, is more biting in Paris than elsewhere. The gayest of cities, it has the farthest to fall in its descent to sorrow. The wittiest of cities, the more noticeable it is there when the joke is flat. The most hospitable of cities, it is the loneliest when the doors are shut. The most openly loving of cities, it is the coldest when the lovers are driven indoors. Here it is impossible to overlook the unheroic fact that not enough people kiss in the rain or at five degrees below zero.

All this is true. And then—
And then the sun comes out.
For two hours, around noon, winter is gone, nobody has ever heard of it. Everybody, somehow, is out and seated at a café table in the open air at chairs and tables that somehow have blossomed there. It is the middle of February, but an amateur botanist can *feel,* in his own blood, the beginning of buds on the trees. Somehow a whole new abundant crop of children between the ages of two and six seems to have been produced overnight, and they are on their way, charmingly dressed and accompanied by the most glorious of young mothers, to the park. Men can be seen hurrying from their offices with tennis rackets in their hands. A sail appears on the Seine. A boy with a beard kisses a girl in blue jeans on a bridge. There is a restaurant that miraculously has a plate of fresh asparagus on the table in the middle of the room. Next to you somebody says he saw the greatest movie of his life the night before and that it was made by a friend of his who is only twenty years old and who borrowed the money to make it from his girlfriend's father. On the other side of you somebody says he is going to Greece for the summer. The boy from Mississippi tells you he has just sold his first short story, and the

hat-check girl says she is going to be married in June. The American who is your good friend and who has been paying alimony for seven years calls to tell you that he has just heard that his ex-wife was married the day before in Las Vegas and you must save the afternoon, the evening, and the night to celebrate with him. A jockey you know whispers about a fantastic workout of a two-year-old that morning at Chantilly and you carefully note the date of the two-year-old's next race. The girls parading before your table shake off their scarves and their hair glitters in the sunshine.

Somebody buys a drink for a young man with a mustache because he has just finished his military service and has been promised a job with Air France. Somebody else claps another young man on the back because he has just beaten the Austrians in the downhill and the giant slalom and you are pleased to see the young man orders milk instead of Pernod. It turns out that the girl with glasses near the entrance, with her eyes closed and her head tilted back, taking the sun, has just completed the definitive work on Bergson and that she has terrified her professors with her erudition. You overhear someone saying a good word about Americans and you read that President de Gaulle is going to speak that evening, and you are reminded that there is one giant, courageous as Ajax and cunning and merciless as Ulysses, left over from the old great age and that he lives in the heart of Paris.

While the sun shines, you think like a Parisian and know why it is so difficult to get him to live anywhere else. He is at the center of the world here. While London is gray because it is uncertain about whether it can live up to its past and Washington is frantic because it is uncertain about whether it can live up to its future, Paris is glittering because it is triumphantly certain, despite all the overt evidence to the contrary, that it is living up to its present. No success really counts, a Parisian thinks in his secret heart, unless it happens in his city, and no failure is really mortal until it has been ratified here. This concept is the height of egotism and demonstrably untrue, and Parisians live happily by it. No joke is funny if it doesn't make Paris laugh, no woman beautiful if she doesn't make Paris send flowers, no dress worth wearing if Paris hasn't sewn it or had it copied, no play a masterpiece if it hasn't pleased a Paris audience, no man a lady-killer if he hasn't broken Paris hearts, no reputation secure unless the hero's name is known by every Paris concierge.

While the sun shines, you go along with the cliché-makers: Paris *is* a beautiful woman, but so surpassingly so, so vital and self-renewing, that nothing—not the passage of years, not drink or drugs, not bad investments or unworthy loves, not neglect or debauchery—can ruin her.

Not while the sun shines. . . .

Within Walking Distance

*T*HE last street I lived on was between the Invalides and the Eiffel Tower and has spoiled me, I'm afraid, for living anywhere else in Paris or, for that matter, in any other city. It is with regret that I must speak of it in the past tense. Where it emerged in the direction of the Boulevard Saint-Germain, after losing itself momentarily in the wide space of the Esplanade des Invalides, the street was an artery into the heart of Paris, bordered by great mansions with sweeping courtyards, where embassies and ministries were installed and luxurious and hidden apartments looking out on miniature parks could be imagined behind the thick guardian walls. It was heavily policed, unencumbered, and made you conscious of the hush of wealth and the manipulations of government as you trod the sidewalks.

The humbler section of the street that I regarded as my own turf was very different. On it there was the variety and human hurly-burly of shops and inhabitants that has lately found favor as the ideal expression of a modern urban society. On the same block, which stretches perhaps a hundred and fifty yards between one wide avenue and another, there were three cafés, two butcher shops, a wine merchant, a delicatessen, an Algerian grocery store, a dairy that was stocked with some hundred cheeses, two hardware stores, a picture framer, a garage, a studio for the renting and repair of movie and broadcasting equipment, two antique dealers, one of them specializing in cutlasses and binnacles, a shoemaker, a laundry and dry cleaner, a man who made overstuffed furniture by hand, a book, magazine, and newspaper vendor, a place to buy infants' clothes, a small, quiet nightclub, a perfume manufacturer, a fruit and vegetable market, two bakeries, a banklike institution that traded in rare stamps, and a travel agency that could arrange a voyage up the Nile or a visit to Yosemite National Park in the space of ten minutes.

All this ground-level commercial bustle was conducted in comfortable 1900s buildings whose modest apartments on the upper stories housed many of the street's shopkeepers and from whose windows could always be seen an old lady or two accompanied by an unpedigreed dog or pampered cat, both peering out, keeping tabs on the activities of the quarter.

On fine summery days, on a tiny balcony that faced my apartment, an aging American couple, who when young were labor organizers with Walter Reuther in the Midwest, could be seen tapping on typewriters as they worked on a book about secular carvings in the churches and cathedrals of France, lost in a Gothic reverie that had nothing to do with closed shops, cost-of-living allowances, or retirement pay.

Parking was illegal because of the narrowness of the thoroughfare, but that did not mean that the way was free of traffic. Motorists cluttered the street with their vehicles, gambling that they had guessed the day or the hour when *contraventions* would not be put under their windshield wipers by the police or their uniformed, sober-faced female adjuncts. On two occasions, upon returning late at night to find the entrance to my own garage blocked, I neatly broke off the side mirrors of the cars parked there, to intimate to the trespassers that wanton disrespect of the rights of innocent passage of Americans was not to be tolerated. I am glad to say I never saw those particular cars again.

On a happier note, the café on the corner served good beer on draft and a Muscadet that could take the enamel off your teeth. The café was also a *tabac*, and with your Havana cigars you could get postal stamps there as well as a nourishing quick lunch at a price that the students, young soldiers, small shopkeepers, artisans, house painters, clerks, and stenographers who kept the café full of life from seven in the morning till ten at night could afford. If you were pressed for time, you could also buy a watch there or a get-well card. If you needed further amusement, you could play table football or try your skill at one of the two garish pinball machines. It also had a telephone, convenient for husbands who preferred to make certain calls from somewhere other than their own homes. You could speak Spanish there and be understood, and after seven years the owner had proudly mastered the words "Hello" and "Good-bye" for our own private use.

To acknowledge my presence on the street, whenever the French translation of a book of mine came out, the owner of the shop at which I bought my newspaper, who had never greeted me by name, put the volume in the middle of his display window, a silent literary signal to the less thoughtful managers of bookstores in neighborhoods where I have lived in America.

If you were willing to leave the street proper, a few steps brought you to the tables of any one of about twenty restaurants, some of them very good indeed. Along with one of the best Chinese restaurants in Paris, there was a busy, low-priced bistro where on fair days you might sit outside at small tables overlooking a carved stone fountain and sample the horsemeat and honest Beaujolais that were featured on the menu. Across the little plaza from it was a restaurant decorated like an 1890 bordello, complete with winding staircase made for the best display of the merchandise as it descended. A hundred yards from what used to be my front door there was a hole-in-the-wall Northern Italian restaurant that had become so deservedly popular with the *cognoscenti* that it was wise to order a table a day in advance; the *insalata di frutti di mare* and the *fondue Piemontese* were well worth the telephone call and the walk. Also within easy reach was a bar devoted to the wines of Sancerre and a solid and fashionable Burgundian restaurant where you feasted off *oeufs meurette*, eggs poached in a red wine sauce, flavored with garlic, herbs, and bits of bacon, and washed down with some of the best vintages of the Côte d'Or. All these flourished, amid a host of others, almost every one of them guaranteed to improve your outlook on life and increase your waistline.

If you preferred to dine at home, you could shop in the nearby market, a thoroughfare of Breughelian copiousness, making your way past carts packed with oranges, lemons, grapefruit, melons, grapes, avocados, apples, pears, strawberries, and flowers. From the tightly packed delicatessens with whole smoked salmons in their windows came the odor of roasting chickens and hot *choucroute* to compete for your favor with the briny smell of ocean from the fish counters and the earthy kitchen-garden perfume of thousands of heads of lettuce and bunches of radishes, leeks, and celery. Even if you were on your way to a restaurant, your eyes and nostrils would be so assailed by the homely beauty and fragrance of Nature's bounty that a stroll through the market would be guaranteed to send you to your meal ravenously hungry.

For festive occasions you could visit a shop on a street three minutes away on foot, where you could find

Tío Pepe sherry, crystallized ginger, Dutch Hopjes, bitter chocolate, and fresh, juice-spurting lichee nuts from the mainland of China. Pineapples, which used to be rented out as centerpieces by hostesses for their more formal dinners and returned the next day, could also be bought at all seasons in this gourmet's retreat, at what seemed reasonable prices.

It was no neighborhood for a man who was fighting the weight, the booze, and the cost of living all at the same time.

For other necessities or pleasures, the quarter offered a large and usually empty movie palace, which sometimes showed films suitable for family viewing, and next to it an English pub, which must have looked like a wonderful investment to some venturesome financiers but which failed and left its mahogany trimmings and advertisements for British ale, Irish coffee, and Pimm's cup to the spiders. If you needed a haircut or a permanent, you could have your choice among a half-dozen coiffeurs and beauty parlors, most often with only one or two barbers or hairdressers working behind plate-glass windows that contained alarming photographs of young women and young men who had allowed themselves to be disfigured by fevered hair stylists who had been driven to these hirsute excesses by human vanity and the lust for novelty of a younger generation with plenty of money in their wallets.

For me, at least, there were better ways of spending money than having my hair done in such a manner that I looked like a Russian ballet dancer or a friend of Napoleon III. Without the need of taking a taxi or a bus, I could buy a heavy-duty valve for a large, incomprehensible machine, a terra-cotta pot for an orange tree, a diamond ring, a bad original painting, a wicker basket made by the blind, a bet on a horse, a waffle from an open-air stand, corks and a gadget to bottle my own wine, beach chairs, a tennis racket, tennis shoes and football cleats, engraved cards announcing my wedding or change of address, a rope to tie together heavy bundles or to hang myself with, a knife for opening oysters, a system to foil burglars, a typewriter or a computer, a seat at a small theater that put on avant-garde plays, the use of a washing or Xerox machine, the services of a dependable student who advertised on a small card in the pharmacy that she would live with me in exchange for taking care of any children I might have, a pizza to take out, a pan that could be placed on the top of the stove and leave marks on steaks as if they had been grilled, utensils for the manipulation of cooked snails, a Larousse encyclopedia, a bathtub, and a coffin.

I could also buy, wholesale, grosses of canned peas and string beans or take a course in Cordon Bleu cooking or enroll for a course in modern literature at the conveniently located American College. If I were so minded, I could have photographs of any banquet I sponsored taken, developed, and distributed to my guests. I could have pamphlets of any description printed around the corner or buy the London *Times*. If I had an ear for music I could hear a string quartet playing Mozart and Schubert in the church not far from the police station. I could buy children's furniture or students' briefcases or a bicycle. Secondhand cars, foreign and domestic, were at hand for my inspection. If I happened to want a passport for Rumania, all I had to do was saunter over to the embassy of that country, nicely stocked with an imposing array of broadcasting equipment on its roof and its windows grilled like a prison, although relations seem to be cordial between France and that Latinized nation, possibly because of the fact that it is the only Communist country that meets France on the rugby field.

I could hire a car with a chauffeur if I thought I would get drunk at dinner and did not wish to take a breatholator test, and get a pair of tickets for the theater at only a slight increase over what it would have cost me if I took the trouble to go all the way across town to stand in line at the box office. I could sell my old furniture without moving from my living room, or drop in on a dealer who would either buy whatever real estate I happened to own or be prepared to sell me any one of a hundred choice apartments on his list.

If, for any reason, I was temporarily not able to use my own apartment, there was a gamut of hotels of all degrees of luxury where I could put up for a week or two, surrounded by traveling salesmen, North Africans, American students, hiking English youths, Portuguese workmen, lilting Indians, doubtful ladies, military men on ambiguous visits to the Ecole Militaire, and dangerous-looking men who slept all day and emerged, looking more dangerous, at night.

You did not have to go out of the neighborhood for funds as there were four or five banks at hand, one of which had been robbed in broad daylight, provoking a wild eighty-mile-an-hour chase through crowded streets and across the Seine, where the shoot-out ended with the killing of one of the thieves and the recovery of the loot in the eighth arrondissement, which, with its jumble of cinemas, clip joints, and flashy clothing stores, is perhaps a more fitting place to be shot by a policeman than the sober street on which the ravaged bank was located.

That is not to say that my neighborhood was at other times completely free of crime. The till of the small Italian restaurant I frequented was skillfully emptied of two days' receipts while the owner and his staff were having lunch in the alcove near the kitchen. There was considerable cash in the till, but since a good many of the payments for food and drink were made by personal check and the owner knew almost every one of his clients by name, a few telephone calls made it possible to have the checks stopped and new ones written to compensate the poor man, at least partially, for his loss. A short time after the deed was perpetrated (the owner hinted, with dark Italian rancor, that he knew who the criminal was) the restaurant was shut down for alterations. When it reopened, the bar and the till were safely in the back, in full view of the kitchen.

My own apartment, modest as it was, also proved to be subject to the age's growing lawlessness. It was broken into twice in my absence—the first time embarrassingly, as I had to explain to the detective on the case that absolutely nothing had been taken. As he inspected the little triangle of glass that had been neatly cut out of the pane near the handle of the door that led in from the terrace, the detective nodded, as though this were an old story to him.

"It's strange," I said. "After all, there was a typewriter, a portable radio-phonograph, a small television set, a drawer full of table silver . . ."

"The man who did the job," the detective explained

to me, "is a professional. His room is probably stacked with sixty typewriters and television sets and sets of silver. He is interested only in money and jewelry. All he had to do here was take one quick look around to see that he was wasting his time."

I have made another enemy, I thought, in yet another profession. I had wasted a hard-working man's time.

"He most likely didn't stay in your apartment more than ten minutes," the detective went on. "We know whom we're dealing with. He makes between three and four robberies a day in this quarter. We have a description. He wears a dark suit and brown gloves and he never leaves fingerprints. And he works only in the daytime, because that is when apartments are usually empty. Also, if he is caught, the penalty is only half of what it would be if he worked at night."

This was news to me. "Why is that?" I asked.

"Because when a thief breaks in at night, the tenants are likely to be present, and in the attempt to deal with the situation there is a strong temptation to violence. The law is severe."

He took me to the police station near the market, on the nearby Rue Amali, where he tapped out my deposition with one finger on an ancient typewriter. This was for the modest claim on my insurance company for what it would cost me to replace the glass on the terrace door, as well as for the police files.

I never heard from the detective again, but the next day a reporter from *Le Figaro* rang my bell to inquire about the robbery, or really nonrobbery. I asked the reporter to keep the item out of the paper, but he merely smiled, and when I bought *Le Figaro* the following morning, the story was there, with my name and address and a description of the building and the floor on which I lived, a useful bit of information for the next illegal visitor, who this time *did* take a tape recorder and a selection of tapes which revealed that he was a collector of light music and had no use for Beethoven or Mahler.

The Rue Amali figured in the news some years later, when the hunt was on for the man called Carlos, a South American terrorist who was reputed to have been involved in the hijacking of airplanes and the bombing of embassies of several countries. When two policemen, guided by an informer, sought him out, he shot the three men point-blank and fled. Later it was discovered that, with a sense of playful irony, he had hidden in a flat on the Rue Amali, just a stone's throw from the police station. When last heard of, he had shot and killed one of the Arab ministers of the OPEC during a meeting of that body in Vienna who had mistaken him for an Israeli. He had taken hostages who were released only when he and his accomplices were given safe plane passage to Algiers. He was photographed, smiling, surrounded by dignitaries of the country, as he landed at the airport.

Another, less violent drama, more in the style of Balzac than of Ian Fleming, was also played to its tragic end on the side of the street across from mine, where there was a store that dealt in a wide variety of foodstuffs, the staples sharing the crowded shelves with more exotic fare such as *pâté de merle, pâté de faisan,* English biscuits, turtle soup, *bisque de homard,* fat, garlicky sausage, sacks of fresh walnuts, oversize succulent prunes, and strings of chocolate wafers wrapped in gold foil to look like minted coins. For the American trade, which was small but profitable, there were Corn Flakes and pancake flour and bourbon whiskey. As in almost every establishment that sells food of any kind, a selection of wines was on view. For the children of the neighborhood, candy was sold by the piece for a few centimes from huge glass jars ranged against the walls, where luscious macaroons and delicious ginger cakes were on display to tempt the youthful appetite.

On lucky Sundays, the proprietors cashed any checks I might have won in the weekly Saturday-night poker games on the Ile Saint-Louis, even when the checks were for daunting amounts. This was more than a convenience, since even if the banks had been open, they were forbidden by law to cash French checks for foreigners who were not legal residents of the country. As several of the pigeons in the game, who loyally tried to fill inside straights week after week, were French and not permitted to have foreign franc accounts, it is easy to understand my chagrin when the store sold out its rich stock of food and drink and closed down.

The drama in this thriving small emporium began rather than ended with a death. The shop had been owned by an elderly but energetic man who made the deliveries, uncomplainingly carrying crates of bottles up steep, narrow staircases and unloading heavy sacks and cartons of canned goods from trucks. He was aided by his son and daughter-in-law; and while they had the worried and slightly apprehensive look that distinguishes most French shopkeepers, as though they feared that their suppliers had unloaded decaying merchandise on them at monopolistic prices, they were courteous to their clients and with each other and the old man, and even managed a nervous little phrase of congratulations to me when I came in—not often enough for my taste—with my poker checks. They worked from seven in the morning till eight at night, on their feet and going up and down the stairs to the storage room in the cellar innumerable times each day. Their only rest was on Sunday afternoons and Monday mornings. By modern standards of working hours and hard physical labor, they put in a great deal more effort than any French factory worker, but they gave the impression of being content with their own small personal domain. Perhaps it was because the profit from their enterprise was theirs to do with as they pleased. Perhaps, and more likely, it was the humanizing aspect of their partnership—making their own decisions, enjoying the opportunity to chat with their neighbors and be treated as people, not as cogs in some abstract machine—that kept their tempers serene and the long hours worthwhile.

Then, suddenly, the old man died. For once the store was closed on a weekday.

It was then that the trouble began. The old man, it turned out, had left his estate to be divided among the couple who tended the store and another son and daughter.

Enter Balzac.

No sooner was the old man buried and the filial tears shed and dried than began that most familiar of French disputes—the struggle over the inheritance. The daughter and the other son, who, as far as I knew, had never set foot in the store and had never sold a pound of sugar or a liter of wine in their lives, asserted claims to the property that my friends, the check cashers, swore they could not live with. Cousins, *notaires,* lawyers, priests, distant relatives, wise men from the town of Albi, where the family originated, all were brought in to dispense justice. To no avail. After months of argument, persuasion, and threats, all sides stood where they had been on the day the will was opened.

On a doomful morning, the sad sign, "A Vendre," appeared on a piece of white cardboard in the store's window, and the place began to take on the appearance of an establishment that had been looted by invading troops as the red-eyed couple sold off cases of wine, stacks of sardine cans, jars of pâté, cartons of tasty English biscuits, at disastrous prices. No one came forward to buy the good name, the solid reputation, the favorable location, the profitable lease, perhaps because the inheritors refused to agree what these imponderables were worth; and finally, with all the shelves bare, the store was shut down and the couple, who were by then my good and pitiable friends, fled to Albi to attempt to start a new business there.

The premises stood vacant, an eyesore in the neighborhood and a reproach to the structure of the nuclear family, for more than a year. Eventually it was reopened as an open-air fruit and vegetable market, featuring esoteric items like New Zealand kiwis and kumquats and fresh red dates, but it was never the same. Although they, too, were open on Sunday mornings, I never had the heart to ask the new owners to cash a check for me.

Although the business of living from day to day, well or ill, commands first attention, intellectual pursuits are not neglected in the quarter. In one of the gleaming new apartment houses on the avenue leading from the Seine, an internationally feared legal expert and theoretician with a beautiful American wife writes cautionary prophecies of what will happen to the world's economy if present tendencies continue. Around the corner, a young scientist who used to be known as the best dancer in France, can tell you all about the newest experiments at the Institut Pasteur, where he works and where things called quarks and charms are being studied. A charm at this moment is believed to be the most minute element of matter in existence, and a quark consists of *three* charms, one positively charged, one negatively, and one neutral.

As far as my limited ability to follow such mysteries is concerned, these are the binding forces that keep everything—stone, flesh, grass, water—from becoming unglued and exploding into inconceivable chaos. It is a long way from my college chemistry course, where I was taught that the atom was the smallest indivisible unit in the universe and that there were only ninety-two of them. I have not inquired how far behind the Institut Pasteur the chemistry classes of the Sorbonne are today.

The dancing young scientist will also discourse learnedly on the engineering of genetic material and holds out hope that in five years or so the research in this field will have gone far enough to control, by the creation of new living compounds, viruses that are responsible for a multitude of human miseries. He will then look at his watch and remark that he must leave now, as he has a train to catch for the weekend's skiing.

For a while it looked as though the Institut Pasteur, with all its illustrious history, would have to close its doors, much like the Casino de Paris, and for the same reason—lack of funds. But the government came to the rescue and now subsidizes the Institut for up to fifty per cent of its running costs, the other fifty per cent being taken care of by the manufacture of vaccines, which should give pleasure to the man who gave the Institut its name, wherever he is.

Ladies who are concerned about the position of women in the world of science can take heart in learning that about half of the researchers at work there are female. In a city that has seen the names of women from Madame Pompadour through Eve Curie dominate different fields of endeavor, this should astonish no one.

There must be a horde of intellectuals secreted behind the buzzers that open the front doors of the quarter's buildings, since so many of the people, men and women alike, whom you pass in the street *look* desperately bookish and intelligent, although with the French you can go very wrong when you make a guess about physical appearances and styles of dress. Beards abound, high foreheads are everywhere, piercing, analytic glances are common characteristics, men and women sit over their coffee in cafés for hours, jotting an occasional note on scratch pads that might or might not contain a line of apocalyptic verse or a reminder to buy a half-kilo of hamburger. There is no telling. The neighbor you are looking at might be an organic chemist or a butcher having his lunch. Unlike America, in France the outward signs of thought are considered socially acceptable phenomena.

When the horses are running in Paris, which is a good part of the year, a Jaguar appears on the avenue, coming up from its underground garage, driven by an

American in his late sixties, dressed in fine dark clothes topped by a black slouch hat. For one incredible day, when he was a lieutenant commander in the American Navy—although that heroic branch of our armed services did not have any craft nearer the Port Maillot than Cherbourg—he found himself, by a freak of organization, our military ruler of Paris, and was the one man who could direct me to the hospital where a private in our outfit was lying after being wounded in an air raid. A Francophile and a lover of horses, he was instrumental in restoring racing as an essential feature of the Paris scene. Close-mouthed, a man of rigorous probity, he has the run of all the tracks, including the sacred precincts of the jockeys' dressing rooms. As he arrives with two or three smartly dressed ladies, whom he ritually picks up at fixed points en route to the track, his car is waved in deferentially to the best parking places near the grandstands. He rarely bets, although there is a constant stream of trainers and jockeys' agents who come to his box or where he is standing in the paddock to whisper into his ear. On the other hand, the ladies who accompany him bet with abandon, usually with no more success than someone who has never seen a saddle and makes his choices with a Ouija board. So much for inside information.

There was no inside information to be had at the café on the corner of the Avenue Bosquet and the Rue du Champ de Mars, which had a betting cage for the patrons of the P.M.U., the Pari-Mutuel Urbain, the organ of the government that runs the off-track betting for all the races in France. In the café there was only hope, calls for divine guidance, and suspicion of all journalists who wrote about racing. The local zeal for plunging had been fanned within the memory of man by the coup of one of the waiters, who had won sixteen thousand francs on a *tiercé* bet of three francs and who then had sworn off all gambling for life.

Observing that I was not averse to a flier from time to time, the owner of the café had attempted to lure me into a poker game with a group of his friends. But French poker has a tendency to be so wild, with so many tricky variations, that I had sensibly declined, feeling rightly that being dealt hands under unfamiliar rules while encircled by a table full of Frenchmen who knew each other's bluffs by heart could only lead to impoverishment.

The café itself, with its two rows of tables on the sidewalk, was the best place to get the full flavor of the neighborhood. It was the meeting place for the teen-age students of the nearby school, boys and girls roaring up on one-cylinder *bicyclettes,* loud but capable at best of thirty kilometers an hour, the girls sometimes achingly beautiful in their embroidered blue jeans, the boys often bearded, with unkempt long hair dripping out of their crash helmets and not worthy, in my eyes at least, of the kisses showered upon them by their female companions.

Because of the jumbled nature of the neighborhood, it was a marvelous place to sit and people-watch, which, after war, is the most ancient of human amusements. There were always children, playing with dogs or dashing by furiously on minute bicycles equipped with two small extra rear wheels that could be detached when the rider grew sufficiently or became expert enough to no longer need the additional support.

There were smartly turned out army officers striding by, briefcases under their arms, in good shape even if they spent their days at a desk. There were tall, beautiful black African ladies sweeping along in gorgeously colored flowing robes and turbans. There was a man with a grotesque goiter who made you feel grateful for your own comparative good health. There were ambulances, their sirens going, on their way to accidents, comforting you in the realization that you were going nowhere that day by car. There were buses, sparklingly clean, uncrowded and with no disfiguring airbrush graffiti, that with a change at some junction here and there could take you on a pleasant, unhurried tour of the city. There were housewives, holding the hands of brightly dressed infants, going shopping. There was an abundance of pregnant young women, proclaiming faith in the future of France.

Late in the morning, ladies who looked as though they had stepped out of a perfumed bath and the pages of *Vogue* at the same time, adorned the avenue, on their way, you supposed, to flirtatious lunches.

There were boys in sweat suits dribbling basketballs or footballs and plump girls in tennis shorts with rackets stuck in the bags behind the saddles of their bicycles. There were one-armed men with decorations in their buttonholes to remind you of a war you had survived.

Across the avenue you could see dark men handling giant earth-moving equipment like toys, under reassuring signs that they were working to improve the justly maligned Parisian telephone system. At two o'clock, when *Le Monde,* always dated for the following day, arrived at the newspaper store a few doors away, you could see distinguished-looking gentlemen reading the paper as they walked, shaking their heads at what they saw on the front page.

The many Chinese and Vietnamese restaurants of the neighborhood added an Oriental touch of color as the cooks and waiters hurried past to their jobs, as smooth in their gaits as though they were on wheels. In the café itself, stenographers whispered hurried lunchtime professions of love to undernourished young men who themselves had only an hour to spare. At the bar itself, there was always the standard drunk or two, voices hoarse and face veins broken by years of honest drinking.

Occasionally there would be a few tourists, somehow lost on the way to Napoleon's tomb, menus in hand, asking each other in English or German or Dutch if they knew what a *croque-monsieur* was. Or there would be a large, bubbling American family with children of all sizes, happy to be abroad, the grown son carrying a full carton of beer, heading for a picnic on the wide lawns of the Champ de Mars. And always the waiters and waitresses hurrying through the traffic with big baskets of long loaves of hot, sweet-smelling bread from the bakery facing the café, and the hairdressers in their white smocks jiggling gracefully across the pavement with trays of small cups of black coffee for their colleagues in their places of work.

The spectacle of two policemen, dismounted from their patrol wagon to give a ticket to a violently protesting motorist, was always well-attended, especially if the motorist was a woman. And everyone watched approvingly as a young cop, dressed like a mechanic, deftly immobilized a car that had been parked in front of the café for three days and three nights by locking a yellow iron contraption to a wheel, thus ensuring that the car's owner would have to report to the police and pay his fine.

In every city there are people who wander the streets

talking and gesticulating to themselves, and the street had its share of those, adding an invigorating touch of madness to the usual strict sanity of the thoroughfare. On one memorable occasion, a shapeless old lady carrying a bag of trash and old newspapers, infuriated that the prim middle-aged woman in front of her paid no attention to her conversation, kicked the offending pedestrian smartly in the calf of the leg. The tolerant spectators intervened to prevent the police from being called, and the shapeless old lady, cuddling her ragged bag, went her way, orating.

There was an institute for the blind a few doors down, and patrons of the café were able to show their fundamental goodness of heart by jumping up from their tables to guide some poor soul with a white cane across the avenue. One blind young man was left to find his way alone, especially by the girls, because his darkened libido drove him to use his free hand very freely on his momentary companion, while he whispered obscene invitations to his room.

The American College, a seat of learning near the river, added its complement of youthful charm to the place, as did the Cordon Bleu School down the block. There, at shocking prices, students from all over the world—including a significant sprinkling of Japanese—tried to learn the secret of how to make *beurre blanc* and roll out *mille-feuilles*. The students spent their off-hours at the café tables, with their books before them, comparing notes on the preparation of *canard à l'orange* and *ris de veau,* deadly serious, criticizing each other's work ("Too much flour in the sauce, kid"), oblivious of the fact that the cuisine of France was generally being reformed in the direction of simplicity.

There were a few older men and women among them, the women most often there for the purpose of tempting husbands, the men with professional aspirations in the kitchens of their native lands. One lady, now graduated, has gallantly opened an outpost in the wilds of Montana and, according to all reports, is doing well. Another student, an American boy of nineteen from Connecticut who yearned to be a great pastry chef, steadfastly refused to learn a word of French, declaring that his whole purpose in life was to be the top pastry chef in Connecticut. He spoke of the man who did the teaching in his chosen field in tones of awe and wonder such as a young outfielder might use in describing Willie Mays. The lower knuckles of his left hand were usually ornamented with band-aids to attest to his zeal in learning the fine points of cutting various vegetables expeditiously into wafer-thin slices with a knife as sharp as a razor.

To combat the influence on my eating habits of these seminarians of *haute cuisine,* when I had dined too well the night before, I made a point of seating myself prominently in view at one of the café tables, ostentatiously lunching off nothing more than a single ham sandwich and a glass of red wine. The fact that the bread was the most delicious in the world—a quarter of a generously buttered, freshly baked *baguette* sliced down the middle—did much to relieve the pains of moderation, but the moral satisfaction remained strong.

As sometimes happens, what I had regarded as an innocent pleasure—chatting idly a few times a week with these serious and dedicated young people—contributed to my Parisian downfall. Among their number there was a young and charming English girl, not the prettiest of the lot but not the plainest, either. She was the seventeen-year-old daughter of friends of mine whom I had met in Switzerland and was living in studentlike austerity in a narrow rented room, sharing it with a slightly older girl-friend. I was on the point of leaving Paris for the winter, and my apartment would lie vacant. Mixing generosity with cunning and remembering that the apartment had been robbed twice when it was empty in my absence, I asked the girls if they would like to move in until I returned. Since the kitchen was the best room in the house and extravagantly well furnished with a spankingly modern stove and refrigerator—irresistible, I thought, to budding cooks—they accepted with pleasure, a pleasure that was accentuated for them by the fact that since I was forbidden by my lease to sublet, they could have it for nothing.

In return, I said, I would expect them to keep the place neat, pay for the telephone, and not have any boys staying overnight or indulging in loud parties, as the rest of the small building was inhabited by small bourgeois families who, as far as I could tell, rose at dawn and were in bed by ten o'clock at night and could be expected to complain if there were any undue noise or flagrantly gaudy behavior. The two young ladies swore that they would be models of maidenlike behavior and that the apartment would gleam like an operating theater upon my return, at which date they promised me a feast prepared by most of the advanced pupils of the Cordon Bleu.

What I overlooked, as a man my age is likely to do when dealing with a girl as young as the demure daughter of my English friends, was that whenever I had happened to see her she was surrounded by a cluster of boys.

When I returned after the three months in other

regions, the older girl was gone—for reasons of economy, my demure young friend explained when she came by to welcome me. I neglected to ask her where she was living now. The apartment was neat enough, but I sensed, rather than knew, that some shirts were missing. Although my tenants were gone, my mailbox kept being filled by letters addressed to people I had never heard of, all of them with masculine names. And the phone kept ringing constantly, at all hours of the day and night, the voices at the other end of the wire all male and youthful, rather curt with me for not being able to produce their demure friend instantly. The calls that came in for the young lady after three o'clock in the morning were likely to be drunk or drugged and uniformly abusive.

I was not spared at cockcrow, either. The bell would ring, especially at the beginning of a weekend, while I was in the last sweet moments of sleep. Staggering to the door, I would confront groups of large young Americans and their shaggy girls, all of whom, it was explained, were going to school in various parts of France and had backpacks full of bedding and had fallen into the habit of spending the weekend in Paris, sacked out in various corners of my apartment.

I don't suppose that a commune had actually been set up in my four small rooms, but I'm afraid it was the next best thing. To add to the pain, I received the telephone bill for the time I had been away. It amounted to well over five hundred dollars. There were charges for calls to many distant places on other continents, and the bill was accompanied by a threat to have my service turned off if I didn't pay in two days.

Resolving never to do a good deed again in my entire life, I paid the bill and presented myself at the

Cordon Bleu, where a particularly disagreeable lady behind the desk informed me that she didn't know where my friend was and refused to accept a note I wanted to leave for her asking her to call me at her earliest convenience.

Luckily, the next day I spied her, surrounded as usual by unkempt admirers. As gently as possible I expressed, among other things, my belief that it would be sporting of her to repay me for the telephone bill. I also asked her to return the two sets of keys I had given her, although I was sure that at that very moment there must have been at least a dozen sets jangling in the pockets of young men throughout the city. The young lady promised that she would appear promptly the next morning with the money, and I released her to her troop of admirers.

There was no ring at the door the next morning, and I learned the young lady had left for London to further her career. The only visitor I had that afternoon was my landlady, who had been called again and again by the other tenants in the building to complain about the ear-splitting sounds of rock music that blasted through the structure each night from the sixth floor, the thump of dancing that vibrated through the concrete, the coarse laughter and female giggles that came from the elevator as it rose toward my apartment in the dead of night. What had been going on could perhaps not be described as a public nuisance, but it certainly could be called at least a semiprivate one, and the landlady made it clear that she had strong grounds on which to have me evicted. As an afterthought she brought up the subject of her son, who was on the verge of marriage.

Admitting defeat, I agreed to move before the snow fell.

The last telephone call came from our embassy in Belgium. A polite consular voice asked my name, then said there was a young man who was in need of help and who had suggested that the American government, which protected us all, call me. The young man was put on the phone. It was one of the most constant of the English girl's attendants and by far the least likable of them all, churlish and superior to any unfortunate creature over twenty-one years of age. "I'm in trouble," he explained. "Something happened at the border. The police're holding the feller I was traveling with. He . . ."

"Drugs?" I asked.

"Sort of. It's a bum rap. There was practically nothing in the car. But they won't let me into France. And they took all my money."

Good old France, I thought.

"What I want you to do, Shaw," he said, "is—I mean you know all sorts of old farts in the diplomatic corps and crap like that—I mean, you could talk to them. And guarantee to this feller here that you'd give him back what it costs me for my fare to Paris, if you get the idea . . ."

"It's Saturday night," I said. "Where do you think I could find any diplomats on Saturday night?"

"You could try, for Christ's sake. I'm due in Paris, man. What do you want to do—leave me in goddamn Belgium?"

"Yes," I said.

"You're a big help, man," he said sardonically. "Well, don't be surprised if I pay you a visit one of these days." He hung up. I was sorry he wasn't going to pay me a visit in the next ten minutes.

In the end, after I wrote a letter to the girl's father,

I received a check for the telephone bill, and the girl herself wrote me a decent letter of apology, saying that she guessed she wasn't as smart and grown up as she had thought she was.

With that, I thought the matter was finished and went about making arrangements to leave Paris. But just before the moving men were to arrive, an anguished telephone call came from the neighbor below me pleading with me not to flush the toilet in my bathroom—she was being inundated. Naturally, it was on a Sunday, when plumbers are not out in full force in Paris. Somehow, an emergency crew was found and the flood was stayed.

But the next morning a plumber rang my bell, holding a small plastic bag in his hand. In the bag, glittering like jewels, were the remains of a heavy cut-glass ash tray that had been found in the pipes between my floor and the one below. The plumber advised me to get in touch with my insurance company to handle the costs of the damage.

As I intimated earlier on, there are certain aspects about leaving Paris that do not fill me with nostalgia.

Searle's Paris: III

Update

This "update" is a hopeful yet impossible journalistic attempt to catch up with time, the never-ending battle against fate and change that the man at the typewriter always loses.

There is no writing for the ages about a world in which cities grow and die, messages travel instantaneously, races mutate, inventions multiply, political fashions sweep over whole populations like oceanic tides. Think about a city or two you have known and loved, and try to imagine what you would have said about it twenty years ago. Or might say twenty years hence.

*A*LL cities, with the possible exception of Venice, have the right to change and, for good or ill, Paris has chosen to alter her face and figure in a thousand different ways. An American arriving in town these days, after a twenty-year absence, might feel that his memory had played him false as he searched for the Paris he had once known. And the writer who rereads his description of an earlier city must pay homage to today's truth in adding and subtracting for today's reader.

For example—the sky itself is different, tainted by industrial fumes, only occasionally clear, and pierced by skyscrapers that are even less aesthetically pleasing than the cold towers of America. The automobile factories along the river are now turning out cars that are almost as large as Cadillacs and considerably more dangerous. In an attempt to solve the insoluble problem of metropolitan traffic, streets have become jumbled one-way channels that mysteriously switch direction with the installation of each new prefect of police, so that finding an address is a pitiful wandering through a maze of medieval alleys, the way usually blocked by a truck from which a leisurely driver is discharging, one by one, cases of disgraceful wine.

The big hotels are no longer full of Americans. Instead, the Arabs have the place of honor, followed by the Germans and the Japanese.

Some of the most prestigious of the hotels have been bought by English corporations, and there have been strikes by the staffs who rebelled at the thought that the meals they would serve would be prepared by British cooks.

Translating his francs into their value in dollars, an American feels a pang of shameful extravagance when he pays a check for dinner, and travelers who had grandly ordered chauffeured limousines to the airport now go by bus because, with the connivance of the concierge, that same limousine could cost a hundred dollars from the hotel to the passport control. There is a new airport, named, naturally, after General de Gaulle, even farther out of Paris than Orly, difficult of access and equipped with passageways done in plastic that in less grand surroundings would be called cattle chutes.

Hilton hotels, or reasonable facsimiles, are springing up all over. There is a McDonald's hamburger joint. Supermarkets are thriving. Girls who don't speak a word of English walk around in jerseys with "University of Kansas" printed on their bosoms. Black jeans are out and blue jeans are *de rigueur*. You can appear in almost any restaurant, even some of the most luxurious ones, without a necktie. There are boutiques everywhere, offering outlandish ready-to-wear clothing off their racks. There are no more baskets of watercress at Les Halles. Les Halles itself has disappeared, the old iron pavilions of Baltard pulled down and a huge, littered hole in the ground the only relic of that bustling, all-night, vigorous world that used to be known as the belly of Paris. Les Halles is now at a place called Rungis, a squat, severely modern agglomeration of sheds on the road to Fontainebleau. What was once a nocturnal fair has assumed the appearance and spirit of a military depot. No longer can the owner of a bistro boast that he has done his shopping for the best meat and the freshest vegetables that morning at four o'clock, because nobody would believe him. The robust restaurants that were scattered among the trucks, the barrows, the piles of country fruit at the foot of the Rue de Rivoli have not followed the exiled merchants, but the tens of thousands of rats who grew fat on the wealth of the market have miraculously made the trek to the countryside and are as fat as ever.

Great restaurants have come and gone. The Berkeley, famed for its *écrevisses à la nage* and its clientele of movie people, politicians, and newspapermen, is now a glorified tearoom where ladies who have been shopping gossip over pastries. The Périgourdine, from whose second-story windows you could look out at Notre Dame while you dined in a handsomely dark-paneled room off truffles charred whole in hot ashes, is now nothing more than a run-down neighborhood café. Nobody can afford a whole truffle any more, either there or anyplace else. The restaurant named for the jazz drummer Moustache and cunningly designed by Trauner, one of the world's best scenic artists, which for five years was the meeting place of *tout Paris* and the international jet set, met its Waterloo in what must have been the direst moment in the city's culinary history. Suddenly, as though in an epidemic of extrasensory perception, the word went out that the food at Moustache's had deteriorated. In the space of a week, the phone fell silent, and only a solitary, unchic, and uninformed diner could be seen munching on his defamed nourishment, not appreciating the still charming but gloomily unpopulated décor. The owner departed, soon after his departed guests, and today, as pretty as ever, the restaurant is an unpatronized *brasserie,* subsidized by a brewery.

The owner of Castel's, the club where the prettiest women were taken to dinner and the prettiest and most obliging girls danced all night, was tried for rape. Naturally he was acquitted, but a shudder ran through the hearts of his clients, none of whom had had any reason to think of rape since their first year at the *lycée.* If it could happen to Jean it could happen to *anybody.*

The wrestlers no longer fly through the air and there are no more pickle jars on the bar of the steak place on the *quais* of the Seine. A despondent lady who lived on an upper floor blew up herself and the whole building in committing suicide by turning on the gas in her oven without taking the precaution of extinguishing the stove's pilot light.

Equally tragically, the owner of Les Porquerolles killed himself when, after many uninterrupted years of seeing his name honored with three stars in the fussily exigent Guide Michelin—the only seafood chef in Paris so distinguished—woke up one morning to find that in the new edition all three stars had been taken from him. Where presidents and prime ministers of powerful countries had blandly survived disgrace and gone on to have their photographs in the newspapers smiling and playing golf, a Parisian cook had observed a code of conduct that would have done credit to the most meticulous samurai.

Foreign upheavals have, as a side-effect, increased the variety of foods to be found in the city. With the collapse of the French dominion in Asia and the disastrous end of American intervention, the number of Vietnamese restaurants have multiplied in Paris, and now, in all quarters of the city, there are red- and gold-decorated eating places where petite handsome yellow men and women who would shoot each other on sight in the rice paddies of their native land chat politely as they pick expertly at their exquisite dishes with chopsticks.

The ebb and flow of military strategy has not only had its effect on the rise and fall of eating places in the city. There are no more brave Allied uniforms to be seen in the streets of the city. The temporary buildings in front of the Trocadéro that housed NATO have been torn down, and NATO itself has been ignominiously sent off to Brussels. We are told that we are welcome to defend Paris, but only at a hygienic distance. The French have a *force de frappe nucléaire* all azimuths, which presumably means they have some missiles aimed in the direction of Washington as well as Moscow.

The young French officers are not leaving any more for Indochina (archaic designation!) and in fact are leaving for nowhere, except perhaps for a garrison town in the south, where the troops are demonstrating for longer hair and shorter working hours. In the Ecole Militaire the decision is being made for the last few battalions to evacuate the Chad at the request of the government of that country, not known up to this date as a superpower.

The flags of governments whose location and political

systems are only vaguely identifiable by anybody outside the Quai d'Orsay still fly from the standards along the Champs Elysées to honor visiting presidents or dictators or tribal chiefs or simple mass murderers, who may learn between one course and another of a state dinner at the Palais Matignon that they have been deposed.

And France, which once bestrode the world, rushes abjectly to do the bidding and beef up the air force of any Arab ruler who owns an oil well.

On the Champs Elysées itself, the prostitutes do not bother to walk. In pairs, ensconced in expensive automobiles, they roam the neighborhood on the hunt for customers who have somehow not read the statistics on the rise of venereal disease in France.

With even more courage, gentlemen still seek sexual companionship along the dark *trottoirs* of the richest residential street in Paris, the Avenue Foch, despite the recent fatal stabbing of a young man who had unwisely repulsed the invitation of a particularly sensitive young woman, who was only out to make an honest buck.

For plusher trade, there was, until recently, Madame Claude, who according to the outspoken satirical newspaper, *Le Canard Enchaîné,* would supply you with a lady so *soignée* and well-mannered that you could take her to Maxim's or even to a communion breakfast of the daughter of a friend of yours. At a price. A stiff price, varying with the amount of time you wished to spend with the lady. The oil sheiks, according to the same source, recruited coveys of these compliant, acceptable beauties when they were forced to sally down to the barren wastes of Monte Carlo for the ritual, Aramco-financed fling at the tables.

The newspapers have reported that Madame Claude

has abandoned her romantic profession and, now a respectable public relations lady under her own name, has been tried by a Paris court for income tax evasion. Found guilty, she was fined fifteen thousand francs and deprived of her civil rights, including the right to vote, for three years. It is not known for whom she voted in the last elections.

Her less noted sisters have also shown unamorous signs of restiveness. There has been a sit-down strike in the sacred precincts of the cathedral of Notre Dame by a group of the city's prostitutes to demand gentler treatment by the police and the advantages of Social Security. Their case is under advisement by the government.

It must not be said that everything has gone bad—although a good deal has. On those tennis courts that have managed to resist the onslaughts of the real estate speculators, the chop and the spin have almost disappeared and the players serve, rush the net, and slam overheads à la Jimmy Connors, a change that a student of the game is bound to applaud.

Although the heart of the city is being jealously preserved, on the surface, at least, some of the other-century picturesqueness may have disappeared in the surge toward the year 2000. But we all must remember, at least in paraphrase, the dictum of Charles Dickens— "The more picturesque the neighborhood, the higher the rate of tuberculosis." The new bleak blocks of flats that presently blight the Paris landscape now have, to the approval of the tenants at least, a lower rate of tuberculosis than, let us say, the ghettos of Harlem and St. Louis, not to mention Chicago or Detroit. They produce a good deal of violent crime, but well below our proud national level and for probably the same intractable reasons. If that is the price the city has to pay for a hundred thousand new indoor toilets, it is not seemly for an American visitor to criticize.

The population of the city has dwindled in an exodus to the suburbs, but armed assault has increased alarmingly. Banks are robbed and hostages taken with monotonous regularity, bombs go off almost daily, and there are certain streets at certain hours that it is wise to avoid if you don't want to run the risk of being mugged. In the Métro it has been necessary to post armed guards for the protection of the passengers. It is not only Coca-Cola and American know-how in the handling of bulldozers and computers that the city has borrowed from us.

The C.R.S., the tough special police, are seen with unpleasant frequency, massed on the streets to stop attacks by militant crowds against the embassies and commercial establishments—with especial attention to air line offices—of countries whose policies, internal or external, meet with their momentary disapproval. The tinkle of broken glass being swept up is a common sound in Parisian ears, the result of the irresistible attraction of plate-glass windows for the irate citizenry. Shopkeepers have become adept at hiding their displays with beaverboard and wooden crossbars—hardly conducive to trade or travel.

Protesters of all kinds have widened their fields of activity and have become malevolently expert at the manufacturing and placement of explosives. To complain about the manner of choosing the Prix Goncourt, the most prestigious of French literary prizes, some Parisian lovers of the art of the novel set off a bomb, with the warning of more to come if the eventual laureate did not meet their expectations. I know many writers in New York who are quick to point out error in the awarding of the Pulitzer Prize, but so far they have done nothing more drastic to express their displeasure than write a letter to the *Times*. Different countries, different customs.

Paris, to its credit, has always been hospitable to political refugees and assorted malcontents, often to its own profit, but this new martial tactic by some of the city's guests has led to the asking of various painful questions by the inhabitants on the nature of the relations between guests and hosts.

The question of the relation of punishment to justice has been hotly debated in recent years, and while prosecutors in murder trials still demand the guillotine, in practice the machine has fallen into disuse. There have been one, or rather two, exceptions, when the guillotine was erected and performed its task in the courtyard of La Santé prison. Two murderers who had killed a nurse and a social worker in a jail infirmary demanded to be executed. If not, they promised publicly to kill again at the first opportunity. Reluctantly, Pompidou acceded to their wishes and they were duly beheaded. More recently, the principal in a particularly ugly murder in Marseille, was also despatched in the traditional manner. Whether this represented an advance or retreat in the administration of justice must be left to the various parliaments of the world to decide.

If American reporters treated crime in the manner of French newspapers, almost all capital cases would be thrown out of court on the first day, on the grounds that a fair trial would be impossible, since as soon as a suspect is apprehended by the police, the headlines read, "Assassin Caught!" The word "alleged" does not seem to belong to the vocabulary of Parisian journalism, and it is light-years away from the prim British formula, "A six-feet-two man in a blue sweater is being sought by the police to help in the investigation."

On the plus side, as the result of an edict by André Malraux, made when he was de Gaulle's Minister of Culture, the centuries of grime have been removed from the façades of the city, amid cries that the ancient dark beauty of Paris was being destroyed. The cries have died down now, as building after building was revealed in white splendor and whole areas took on a youthful lightness of color when the cleansing process was completed. A section of the Marais, a neighborhood of exquisite eighteenth-century mansions that had been allowed to deteriorate into a slum, has also been restored in all its formal symmetry, and plays and concerts are given nightly in the summer against a background of noble walls and gleaming tall windows.

Paris is a twenty-four-hour-a-day city, and in recognition of this the ancient palaces, the domes, spires, and monuments are now artfully lit after nightfall, making even the grim business of settling lawsuits and condemning criminals behind the stone bastions of the Palais de Justice seem decoratively festive when the rest of the world has gone dark. And the *bateaux mouches,* the excursion ships that ply the Seine, send probing playful beams from their searchlights to catch lovers on the *quais* and husbands and wives in domestic poses in riverfront apartments. A proposed Left Bank motor expressway, approved under the Pompidou régime, has been canceled, a democratic concession by the new man in the Elysée to those most appreciative of Parisians, pedestrians and fishermen.

To cope with the deterioration of one of the most perfect open spaces in the city into a mere parking lot, the government has built a vast subterranean garage under the Place Vendôme, and now, on opposite sides of the generous plaza, at whose center stands the great bronze column, the stately entrance of the Hotel Ritz confronts the equally stately gates of Morgan's Bank— expensive Continental luxury saluting excessive American money across an unencumbered expanse of unmotorized beige gravel. To celebrate the renewal of the clean architectural symmetry of their ancestors, the Escadre Noire of Saumur, performing on their gleaming black steeds, went through a dazzling series of intricate and perilous maneuvers for three summer nights for the delight of the populace.

Continuing the work of Malraux, who sponsored *maisons de culture* throughout the country, new theaters are being built in the working-class suburbs of Paris. I had the good fortune to be present at a performance in Boulogne-Billancourt, where an old play of mine was most professionally revived in a new State-financed theater that was as comfortably appointed as any on Broadway. It had the not-to-be-scorned added attraction of a bar where splits of champagne were served during intermissions. However, I made the mistake of going to the dressing rooms after the final curtain. I found that the lavish use of space and expensive carpeting out front had been compensated for by the architect in a niggardly economy backstage, putting a heavy burden on the ingenuity of the scene designer, as there was no provision for the storing or flying of sets.

"As usual," said the leading actor, a veteran of a hundred first nights, "when they build a theater they never consult an actor."

American plays as a rule do not do very well in Paris, although American movies, both in the original and dubbed versions, are usually popular. In the domain of literature, critics are likely to be lofty, with a few notable exceptions, about American books. To Frenchmen used to centuries of books with limp, plain paper covers, the growing practice of publishing books in hard covers, with colored jackets, is looked upon as a manifestation of un-aesthetic sensationalism, designed to attract the lower-brow trade.

The language of the theater, even if translated literally, would hardly shock even the most prudish American or English visitor, exposed as he or she has been these last years to the barracks-room candor of London and American drama. And dear old Anouilh is still represented on three or four stages each season to demonstrate that the literary flash in the pan is not a common phenomenon in French culture, as, alas, it is in other lands.

A sad note has been struck for nostalgic lovers of the drama in the retitling of the Sarah Bernhardt theater. The name of the tragedienne who had played Hamlet and the leading role in *L'Aiglon* to worldwide applause had remained on the façade of the huge hall on the Right Bank of the Seine even during the Nazi Occu-

pation; but when the theater was refurbished, some per-
suasive, cold-blooded modernist had prevailed upon the
authorities to take down the name that resounded for
generations with so many echoes of the glory of French
drama. Now the spacious auditorium is called Le Théâtre
de la Ville de Paris. Pity the poor lady with the one leg,
who had been the object of so many columns of rapturous
critical prose, who now is finally in the coffin in which
she had spent many curious but peaceful nights while she
was alive.

Across town, on the hill of Montmartre, the Casino de
Paris, another monument, to a less austere but more
popular French art, is also suffering from the winds of
time. The fabled haunt of pleasure, with its splendid girls
in their splendid feathered costumes, its lavish scenery,
its generous display of fulsome sexuality, may soon go
dark. The present director, choreographer Roland Petit—
whose wife, the delicious Zizi Jeanmaire, has been the
star for years of the spectacle—has announced that without outside help, rising costs will force him to close down.
Aging Parisians and their guests from the provinces are
looking pleadingly toward Saudi Arabia as they watch
still another memento of their salad days slide toward
oblivion.

Time has also taken its toll of the men and women
who adorned the theatrical, literary, and sporting scenes
of the fifties and sixties. Jouvet and Gérard Philippe,
those protean actors, are dead, and Piaf's sad chants can
be heard now only on recordings. Mauriac and Cocteau,
passionate antagonists who hurled chunks of prose at
each other like hand grenades, are gone. Sartre is old and
blind, and the torrent of his language has been dammed.

Carpentier is dead, mourned by the media in terms that might have been used in eulogies for the chevalier Roland when the news came through that he had fallen at Roncevaux. Claude Dauphin, suave and sexy matinee idol in boulevard comedies, now plays Shylock and Willy Loman.

The new stars are likely to be rock singers, their electronically amplified rhythms rancorous to ears that had become attuned to a gentler music.

The least costly and perhaps the most satisfactory of Parisian amusements is merely to walk around the city. The idle stroller will observe a minor detail that reflects a major alteration in French thinking. In the pharmacies he passes he will note that fecundity calendars are no longer on display in the windows. For a simple reason: Despite thundering from the pulpits, abortion and the pill are now legal, and as far as one can tell, the women are making the most of it. The women themselves seem to have sprung from another race, taller and more athletic than the original descendants of the Gallic tribes. Part of the increase in height may be attributed to the new habit of drinking orange juice in the morning, and the rest to the four- and five-inch heels on the fetching and at the same time climatically sensible boots that are now worn by almost everybody.

Politically, too, the presence of women has increased. There is Madame Simone Weil in the Cabinet; and at the height of the debate about abortion a large group of prominent women, including many film stars, let it be known in a public statement, complete with photographs, that they had all undergone abortions, even though the law still in force at the time could easily have put them in jail for harsh sentences. French flexibility in the administration of justice was admirably demonstrated by the fact that no charges were brought against these brave pioneers of family planning.

Madame Weil has shown her independence of spirit by inaugurating a vigorous campaign against cigarettes —a delicate political balancing act, since the State has the tobacco monopoly for all France, and a good deal of its revenue comes from the licensed sale of the now officially repugnant weed.

Another woman in high position in the capital, Madame Françoise Giroud, one of the top editors of the magazine *L'Express,* gave notice—not for the first time— that she was to be reckoned with when the magazine, against her objections, published several pages of luridly explicit stills from the pornographic film *L'Histoire d'O.* With ladylike diffidence but with iron determination, Madame Giroud merely removed her name from the masthead of the magazine. For Parisians, ever sensitive to the subtlest of power plays, it was the event of the week.

L'Express was bombed shortly after the questionable issue hit the stands, but it is doubtful that the attack had anything to do with sex. When the managing editor was questioned about his views on the possible allegiance of the perpetrators of the bombing, he merely shrugged wearily and rattled off a list of about twenty clandestine organizations, any one of which was a worthy candidate for suspicion. It is not easy in present-day Paris, especially for a newspaperman, to pinpoint enemies.

The subject of pornography in general has mightily disturbed the councils of state, necessitating full meetings of the Cabinet to deal with it. Until recently, there had been a loose censorship of films, preventing French producers from competing in lubricity with their Scandinavian and German brethren. For example, the showing of actual penetration, that most innocent of acts, was forbidden. Among the liberalizing concepts that Giscard d'Estaing brought into office with him was that all censorship be abolished, and the screens of Paris—and indeed of all France—were inundated with representations of acts of sadism, masochism, sodomy, and other assorted delights that left absolutely nothing to the imagination of the viewer. The public, alas, flocked to the cinemas where these heretofore forbidden entertainments were being shown. In those theaters that still stubbornly played traditional films, even of the highest caliber, receipts dropped disastrously. Adding their cries of anguish to those of bishops and educators, the old-time producers begged for succor. Reluctant to go back on its liberal principles but conscious of the ground swell of indignation among its constituents, the government came up with what must have seemed, around the conference table, a brilliant solution. Censorship would not be reestablished, but everybody involved in the making and dissemination of offending skin flicks would be taxed to a point where it would be economically ruinous to continue.

Unfortunately, this produced another howl of rage from some of the most distinguished directors and actors in France, since this edict could be used as a weapon against films of undoubted quality that might, in the service of artistic integrity, contain scenes that could quite easily be subject to the new tax. Further Cabinet meetings will certainly be held.

It is not only the excesses of the new permissive society that result in calls for emergency sessions on the Rue Faubourg-Saint-Honoré. The government of France, which has its seat there, is rigorously centralized, and any twinge or rumble anywhere in the hexagon has an immediate repercussion in the capital. In the mid-seventies twinges and rumbles have come by the dozen. Unemployment, which was unknown in the fifties and sixties, has been widespread. Inflation has been unchecked. Foreign workers, who form an uneasy and until now shabbily housed and shamefully treated base for the French economy, are organizing, and it is difficult not to sympathize with workmen who often live twelve to a room. The Basques and the Bretons are clamoring for autonomy and the teaching of their separate languages in the State-run schools. In Brittany the central television tower was blown up, perhaps as a just criticism of French television, which is under strict government control. From Paris, of course.

The low quality of French television, which is noted occasionally by even the most conservative of the Parisian press, is due, according to the artists who work for it, to the fact that in the studios there are three executives for every one creative individual who has anything to do with actually putting an image on the screen. On the left, the O.R.T.F. is merely dismissed as a purveyor of pap and a public relations branch of the government in power.

On a warmer front, the growers of wine in the south have poured thousands of liters of Italian wine onto the roads and have taken to shooting at the police to protest the cheap imports from their Latin partners in the Common Market. Strikes are drearily and uncomfortably commonplace. On certain days the trains don't run, or the buses, the garbage is not collected, arias are not sung at the Opéra or *Le Misanthrope* played by the Comédie Française, and riders in elevators are marooned between floors of skyscrapers when the electricity is cut off. There has been a flood of checks issued without funds or against mythical accounts, and drastic measures have been announced to put a halt to this blithe instant banking by consumers who are momentarily or permanently short of cash. New ways are being constantly devised by the brilliant graduates of the Polytechnique who man the government's economic bureaucracy to persuade the canny and evasive French taxpayer to mend his ways and to acquiesce in an act he has never considered reasonable behavior—paying his allotted share of taxes.

Across the river, in the Chambre des Députés, the Opposition on the Left, composed of the Socialist and Communist parties, which only lost the last election by a small percentage of a point, growls and threatens. M. Mitterand, the Socialist leader, is comparatively polite—and adamant. M. Marchais, the leader of the Communists, a man with the most baleful eyes in the politics of any nation now in existence, is most impolite—and adamant. His harangues are so fiery that he is burnt in the heat of his own oratory to such a point that after each speech in the hemicircle his blood pressure has to be taken by an attendant physician.

The urbane and aristocratic man who was elected President of his country deals daily with these and other matters, somehow preserving his urbanity and attempting to play down his aristocratic image by being photographed playing football, by wearing business suits at functions that used to be graced by splendid costumes, by walking up the Champs Elysées in parades instead of riding in a limousine, by having publicized dinners with ordinary citizens in their simple homes, by declaring that November 11 shall henceforth be celebrated as a memorial day for all Frenchmen who have fallen on the field of battle rather than a yearly martial ceremony to mark the defeat of Germany in World War I.

Paying lip service to de Gaulle, the President seems to be consciously edging away from the icy majesty with which his predecessor surrounded the office. In a further effort to wean the French away from the notion of *la gloire,* he has had the "Marseillaise" rescored, demanding that its ringing cavalry-charge rhythms be transmuted into something more sober and fitting for a civilian era.

More concretely, on the political front, to demonstrate that if he is not exactly *of* the people, he is at least in some measure *for* the people, he has signed a law that assures ninety per cent of a full year's pay for any worker who loses his job, a concession to our troubled times that will almost certainly have widespread repercussions throughout the Continent.

Another, less popular, move, that of raising the *tiercé* base price from three francs to five, has horse players grumbling as they punch the ritual holes in their complicated printed tickets each Sunday morning. The *tiercé,* conceived in 1954, a relative of our daily double and the New York City Exacta, is government-run and a highly profitable scheme for raising funds for the *Trésor National.* It is a system in which the bettor picks any number of horses in a designated race, usually one with at least fourteen starters, in the order in which he thinks or guesses or divines or dreams they are going to finish. The winning price for the first three in order can be enormous. There are complex variations that include using the field in bets, which I have never been able to understand although I have seen grizzled taxi drivers and day laborers, armed only with a copy of *Paris Turf* and whose accents betray no signs of higher education, dashing through what seems to me the most arcane mathematical calculations between one Calvados and another in their pursuit of sudden wealth.

Human nature being what it is, the element of chance and the notorious unreliability of horseflesh, plus the huge amounts of money involved, have from time to time been regarded as an open invitation to larceny. When the betting commissioners one Sunday morning noted that an inordinate amount of francs was coming in for a *tiercé* race over the jumps called the Prix de la Bride Abattue on certain combinations of outsiders, their suspicions were immediately aroused, especially since most of the bets were being made in Marseille, the official capital of French gangsterism. Their suspicions were greatly strengthened when at the very start of the race all the favorites fell back into an orderly platoon far behind the group of outsiders and stayed docilely in their wake until the end, a performance that hardly lived up to the title of the race, which translates as "at full tilt." The payoff on the finish and the *tiercé* was suspended, and a long investigation revealed that an arrangement had been made with a number of jockeys to control the order of arrival. The jockeys were arrested, convicted, and jailed, and the State kept the money. To further feed the indignation of the gentlemen who devote their efforts to the improvement of the thoroughbred in France, in the course of the affair it was learned that one of the jockeys had threatened another jockey with death for talking too much. The violent little horseman was given an extra year to remind him to mend his manners.

All the news that emanates from the Bois de Boulogne, where the two leading racetracks of Paris, Longchamps and Auteuil, are located, is not necessarily bad. For some time now, French horses have dominated the tracks of the Continent and England, and bands of hearty English gentlemen and tweedy ladies who come over to Paris for the weekend to put their money where their hearts are have little to celebrate as they watch British champions left behind in the stretch by French colts and fillies in one rich stake after another.

In Paris, scandals are not confined to the paddock. The realm of politics contributes more than its share of flavorsome gossip. M. Mitterand himself, who was just a hairbreadth away from the Presidency, was involved in an outlandish plot in which he was lured into being an actor in a fake attempt on his life by a Right-wing legislator. Real bullets were fired from an automatic pistol, and M. Mitterand made a convincing leap over the walls of the Luxembourg Gardens to add realism to the scenario. In an attempt to bring down his victim by ridicule, however, the Right-wing legislator overplayed his hand a bit by boasting openly about his part in the affair. He, too, was imprisoned for a short period, and M. Mitterand, only momentarily embarrassed, climbed steadily to his present eminence. It is hard to imagine a British MP who dove behind a tree in Hyde Park to evade a fusillade of bullets carefully aimed fifteen feet south of his hiding place, or an American senator dodging behind a pillar at the Lincoln Memorial in a similar charade, going on to become a leader of his party. Poor Wilbur Mills, after a lifetime of congressional probity, was exiled from Washington merely for strolling onstage in Boston where his lady friend was performing in a striptease act. In Paris it most probably would have been regarded as a momentary sentimental aberration, in no way reflecting on Representative Mills's political qualifications.

M. Chaban-Delmas, the mayor of Bordeaux and one-time Prime Minister of France, was not as fortunate as M. Mitterand, his successful competitor at the polls. When it came out that Chaban (as he is called), although a man of considerable wealth, had not paid a sou in income tax for years, the voters rose against him, even after he went on television to make a Checkers-like speech in which he pointed out, correctly, that he had stayed impeccably within the law in making out his returns. His hopes to succeed Pompidou in the Presidency were shattered in the preliminary elections, and his Gaullist party has since fallen into bickering disarray. Money, it turned out, is a much more serious matter to the French than bullets when it comes to putting an ''x'' on a ballot. Chaban was not helped by the Bordeaux wine scandal, either, when some of the most illustrious fellow citizens of the mayor of the city were convicted of sending out what had been regarded heretofore as the most honest of wines under false labels, an act considered in the ancient province of Aquitaine in much the same light as switching babies in a hospital.

Pompidou himself was the object of unsavory rumors after the murder of the Yugoslav bodyguard of screen actor Alain Delon, with whom the Pompidous were said to have dined several times. There were whispers in drawing rooms and echoes in the press, never documented and always changing, of unspecified sexual goings-on that no one who had ever known the couple could ever credit but that persist to this day, long after Pompidou's death.

And there is an unfortunate tax collector for the richest section of Paris, the sixteenth arrondissement, who has languished in jail for years on the suspicion that he looked with an all too lenient eye on the returns of some of his well-heeled contributors, several of whom were figures in the government. An investigation has dragged on for month after month, with no concrete evidence emerging, as investigations have a habit of doing in Paris. The poor man will probably remain behind bars until all dossiers relating to the case have been devoured by termites.

When it was discovered that there was a central building in the city where listening posts were monitored on a twenty-four-hour-a-day basis and the private conversations of almost everybody who was anybody were recorded and overheard by minions of the party in power, there was an uneasy stir for a week or so, and then public attention shifted to more interesting matters. Admirably, Giscard ordered the institution shut down permanently and promised that the practice would cease forthwith. The praise he elicited for this unconventional act was tepid. Parisians openly wondered why we Americans made such a fuss about the Watergate tapes. What else was a politician expected to do? What else *could* he do?

When an elderly and respected high churchman was found dead in the apartment of a lady who was not famous for her virtue, the official story was that he was visiting a parishioner in need of moral uplift. Every Parisian, as usual, had a complete unofficial version of the story, gleaned for the most part from the numerous scandal sheets, whose glaring headlines seem to be printed in racy disregard for whatever libel laws exist in France. On all occasions, there seems to be someone on the inside who is ready to tell what he knows or what he pretends to know to an enterprising reporter with a wallet full of francs. Despite this journalistic freedom—or license, if you will—there has been a marked decrease in the Gaullist practice of hauling editors into court and fining them for making unkind remarks about government figures and policy.

For newspapermen everywhere, the practice that is gaining in Paris of allowing journalists to choose their own editors and to dictate policy, even when the profit from the enterprise goes into other pockets, must seem like a glorious experiment in keeping the stain of commerce off editorial desks.

If the awareness of city dwellers to what is going on in the world around them can be gauged by the number and variety of the newspapers that are available to them, the inhabitants of Paris must be among the best informed in the world. While New Yorkers have to make do with three morning papers, which number includes a fringe sheet like *Women's Wear Daily,* and one evening paper, the *Post,* Parisians can enlighten themselves and keep abreast of almost all shades of social behavior and political opinion in no less than thirteen daily newspapers. While news is not ignored, polemic and rhetoric are not confined to the middle and last sections, as they are in American journals. Prominent space on the front page is as often as not devoted to the sober musings in rich prose of members of the Académie Française on whatever subjects happened to have wandered into their minds at breakfast the morning before, and *Le Figaro* invariably displays the work of the satirist Pierre Daninos across many columns of its front page whenever he is moved to write one of his biting, highly civilized essays.

Any discussion of the newspapers of Paris, no matter how cursory, would be incomplete without mentioning the Paris *Herald Tribune,* solvent survivor of its parent, the late lamented New York *Herald Tribune.* The Paris paper is now called the *"International Herald Tribune,* Published with the New York *Times* and the Washington *Post,"* a combination that gives the lucky editor in the famous tacky office on the Rue de Berri a rich variety of dispatches and journalistic talent to choose from in making up his paper. The result is enough to make a newspaper buff living in New York or Washington sigh with envy, for in a mere fourteen pages, or sometimes even less, the *Trib* on any one day might have Art Buchwald, James Reston, William Buckley, Red Smith, and Waverly Root, that enchanting octogenarian gourmet and quirky historian of the foods we have eaten through the ages. To add luster to the syndicated wisdom of these eminent gentlemen, there is also a handful of other journalistic stars, plus a sprinkling of local news and reviews, all for the price of a single newspaper. The price, it must be admitted, is a stiff one—two and a half francs, which, at the last reading, is about sixty cents—but only the most impoverished of Latin Quarter Americans would dream of going through the day without buying it.

It is possible that through the years hundreds of homesick Americans who had not seen a football game in a decade have managed to bear their exile by the simple expedient of opening the paper to the sports page and reading the rundown of Sunday's NFL scores.

With all its cosmopolitan sophistication and international interests, the *Trib* still manages to maintain a little of the home-town chattiness of a small-town paper, and letters to the editor for and against Parisian manners or Parisian prices are printed with neighborly good humor. When an impolite review of one of my books, culled from the New York *Times,* appeared in the paper, the editor compassionately published a letter of mine in which I was allowed to point out to readers of the *Trib* that the book had been cordially received in other quarters and that one critic did not a novel make. Although I have never written anything for the *Trib* and have contributed occasionally to the New York *Times,* I would never have dreamed of sending such a letter, or any letter at all, to the *Times.* For a simple reason. They never would have printed it.

Searle's Paris: IV

Departure

*Y*OU end at a café table, because everything in Paris ends at a café table.

You are expecting no one to join you. On this day you want to be alone.

The team of three moving men are in the apartment, under the direction of a bald Turkish gentleman. They are rolling out furniture on dollies and packing books, glassware, paintings, and the odds and ends of twenty-five years into large cartons. The one full bottle of Scotch left in the cabinet has been presented to them. They have also drunk all the beer remaining in the refrigerator and have made a selection for themselves of the books in French that were put aside to be donated to the library of the American Student Center. The bald Turkish gentleman has promised that the cartons will be delivered to Switzerland within a week. You do not know at the time that a month later the cartons will still be in Paris and the moving company will be threatening to sue you. The city does not loose its grip on you without a fight.

The Turkish gentleman has fretted about documentary proof, for presentation at the Swiss border, that you actually had a household in France. "You cannot take goods out of France," he says, in Turkish-English, "unless there is evidence that you have resided in France. Where is your *permis de séjour?*"

"I do not have a *permis de séjour*. I have never stayed more than three months in France at any one time, so I didn't need one. Tell the people at the border that I was a tourist."

"It is not sufficient, sir." He shakes his head. "The lease for the apartment, perhaps?"

You shake *your* head. The lease was lost in the scramble of a divorce.

"I'm afraid, sir," he says, "that as far as the law goes you have no legal existence."

It is the first time anywhere that you have been told you had no right to exist.

"Perhaps a signed statement from your landlady to the effect that you were indeed an occupier of the premises?"

You shake your head again. Although the lady has agreed to buy the extravagant kitchen equipment, and happy as she is at seeing you go after the incident of the broken glass in the pipes, you do not think she would be eager to oil the machinery of your departure.

The Turkish gentleman sighs. He had been jovial a few days previously when he had come to make the assessment, had spoken of literature when he saw all the books, had accepted a whiskey. Now that he is faced with the difficulties of French paperwork, there is an Ottoman sorrow in his eyes, the Christians winning, the fall of Islam inevitable. "Still," he says, noting the impatience in your own eyes and seeking a ray of light in the darkness, "it would be worse in Constantinople."

It is small comfort. Between you and the bald gentleman there floats the vision of precious relics, beloved books, paintings by friends who are now being shown in museums, forever remaining in limbo, gathering dust somewhere in the corner of a warehouse, their owner nonexistent.

"Taxes?" he says, without hope, his tone implying that certainly you were too educated to have actually paid taxes.

"Ah," you say. You know that somewhere in the piles of paper still unpacked there should be a bill for an exorbitant amount from the city of Paris, so far unpaid.

You search. You find the sheet of yellow paper with its peremptory demand for two thousand francs and no explanation of how that figure was arrived at. You hand it over.

The sun breaks over the Bosphorus as the Turkish gentleman takes the yellow sheet of paper in his hand. "Excellent," he says.

Magically, taxed, you now exist legally. The French customs men will be pleased.

A friend comes in to pick up a dozen exquisite Baccarat *ballons* that he had been promised as a parting gift. The *ballons* were meant only for the serving of the greatest of vintages—Château Haut-Brion '29, Richebourg '47, Cheval Blanc '19. Anything less would have been an insult to the artist who had created them. They have been used only once. The cook had refused to touch them, saying, "They shatter when you just look at them. I can guess what they cost. I cannot be responsible."

The friend carefully packs the glasses, not breaking any of them. He has a peculiar new expression on his face, one that you have not seen in all the twenty years you have known him. He is a gentle and loving man. You try to keep a word out of your mind. The word is avidity. In even the best of us, you think sadly, a scavenger lurks.

"I hate to see you leave," he says. He means it. "But you will be back."

The boys from the American Student Center come in for their share of the apartment's furnishings. One of the boys is a frail, beautifully grave Indian with long, silken, very black hair. As he speaks, in that peculiarly inflected, careful English, you try to think who he reminds you of. Of course. Peter Sellers. Is it possible that because of Sellers' languages, a half-billion citizens of the subcontinent will always make every English-speaking moviegoer or television viewer think of Peter Sellers?

The boy shyly answers questions. He is a graduate of the University of Bombay, with a B.A. in agriculture and economics. India is in dire need of agricultural and economic experts, but he is here, removing frying pans from a kitchen cabinet in Paris.

He is twenty-six years old, he says, and penniless. He has applied to the University of Wisconsin for a scholarship to continue in his valuable studies. He has received a polite reply: He must be sponsored by his own government. He smiles ruefully. "You must know somebody in the government to be sponsored." He was born with the knowledge of corruption in high places. "I do not know anybody."

He plans to work, if he can, for four years more in Paris, saving his money to go to the University of Wisconsin, where, he has heard, they are strong on agriculture and economics.

The boys cart out the furniture, struggle to get beds through a door, remove a sconce from the wall, assemble books, manhandle the refrigerator, begin to take down the curtains and drapes, start to tear up the carpeting.

It is an hysteria of gathering. The apartment is no longer a familiar place. You decide it is time to go and sit in a café. Alone.

The café you have chosen is not in the *quartier*. You have wanted to put some distance between yourself and the place where you have lived. You have crossed the bridge (do we search for symbols?) and are sitting on the *terrasse* of the café on the Place de l'Alma that Giraudoux used for the *mise en scène* of *The Madwoman of Chaillot*. It is a gray day. The Seine looks wintry. You have sat there in the month of June with a lovely Irish girl, soft in speech and manner, victim of an unhappy marriage. You have not seen her in years. You have heard that she has remarried. You wonder if she is happy.

Memories flood back . . .

Another lady, Marlene Dietrich, old friend from the Hollywood days, just after the Liberation, marching you grandly past the MP's on duty at the entrance of the Ritz Hotel, now a field-grade officer's billet, to take a bath in her suite, because the Ritz is the only place in town that has hot water. Then, in the company of Joe Liebling, who has found a hansom cab somewhere, clop-clopping across the city behind an old horse the Germans had neglected to steal, to the Porte Saint-Martin, where Liebling has made contact with a favorite restaurant of his from before the war, now doing business on the black market, with a good menu and fine wine. Liebling is on an expense account from *The New Yorker,* which is the only decent way to be involved in a war, so you have no compunction in ordering the kind of meal you have been dreaming of while living off K rations on your way to Paris.

To round off the feast, Miss Dietrich, chic in her USO uniform, softly sings a selection of her old songs, over the coffee and brandy.

Miss Dietrich is not the only performer to offer her talent to the troops. Just after V-E Day, as the prize for services rendered, the British Arts Council sends over a company of actors headed by Laurence Olivier. The play is *Arms and the Man* and is given in the beautiful Théâtre Marigny, set in the park of the Champs Elysées;

it is received uproariously by the triumphant troops in the audience, with every mocking Shavian reference to the idiocy of war and warriors bringing thunderous applause.

Less fortunate than the session with Liebling, there is an encounter with another correspondent. You get into a three-handed poker game in the bar of the Hôtel Scribe and on private's pay lose a thousand dollars in an hour to Charles Christian Wertenbaker, courtly Virginia gentleman who worked for *Time* then and later wrote a novel about that phenomenon that did not meet with favor when it was reviewed there. Later, in the new civilian age, there were the trips with him to the bullfights at San Sebastián, Santander, Legrono, Dax, and Bayonne. You also sat on the beach with him at Secoua in the Basque country, where he lived, and drank daiquiris with him and his wife, pouring the Cuban nectar out of a huge glass vase, transported to the beach in an open car through the town of Saint-Jean-de-Luz, from the house on the hill you had rented for the summer and which was well stocked with rum and lemons.

You remember that Wertenbaker, in his final illness, had pointed out the cemetery on the slope overlooking the bay where he was going to be buried.

Other drinks, other conversations. The fifties . . .

Do not forget the dark old bar at the Hôtel Continental, across from the Tuileries, were you had sat the long afternoon with Janet Flanner, talking of Harold Ross, who, you had learned by cable, had just died.

Then there is Alexandre's, on the Avenue George V, where every midnight your American friends would congregate, as in a club, Bob Capa drawling out his Hungarian-accented English, a cigarette drooping from his mouth, saying, "I am not happy." John Huston, in town to make *Moulin Rouge*. Carol Reed, working on his circus picture with Burt Lancaster. Gene Kelly, for *An American in Paris*. Tola Litvak, with his white mane of hair, the ribbon of the Legion of Honor in his buttonhole, a hero in Paris since he directed *Mayerling,* the stunning model who was to become his wife at his side. Billy Wilder, caustically witty, in town for the shooting of *Love in the Afternoon.* David Schoenbrun, speaking impeccable French, full of information and hardly able to wait to make his upcoming broadcast on the sinuosity of French politics for CBS. Art Buchwald, the next day's column just finished, looking for a poker game. Sam Spiegel, plumply groomed, heavy-lidded, multilingual and erudite, his hard Hollywood days behind him, enjoying the success of *The African Queen,* preparing himself with an emperor's assurance for the glories of *The Bridge on the River Kwai* and *Lawrence* and one of the largest yachts on the Mediterranean, with a crew of twenty.

You remember the night when Spiegel and Peter Viertel nearly came to blows at the table because Spiegel thought that Viertel had done him less than justice in the character of the movie producer in Viertel's novel *White Hunter, Black Heart.* All the bets at the table were on Viertel, twenty years younger and a physical fitness devotee, but after a good deal of shouting, peace was restored and the two men are still fast friends.

Everybody was feeling successful and lucky to be there in that fine city, among talented companions, during that energetic period when they were all working hard and doing well and full of projects for the future, carelessly prosperous in that blissful time when the United States government still allowed American citizens on salaries abroad to remain exempt from income tax.

It must not be thought from the above that all Americans in Paris in that era were delighted to be there. The blacklist and the House Un-American Activities Committee had not been forgotten and there were men there in Paris who had had booming careers cut short in Hollywood and New York and were now without passports, living on the sufferance of the French government, hounded, working—if they found work at all—at derisive wages, unable without papers to cross a frontier or sign their work with their own names, knowing that there were informers—hired liars everywhere, even at the jovial table at midnight at Alexandre's—ready to destroy a supposed friend for pay.

Bruised, but only glancingly, by the ignominious antics of the witch hunters, you can afford to be amused when you hear that the librarian at the USIA library in Naples had hurriedly whisked your own books to the safety of the cellar just before the arrival of the famous McCarthy team of watchdogs, Cohen and Schein. An officer in the Foreign Service in the American Embassy, whose only un-American activity was alleged adultery, had the pair of fervent patriots followed and their phone bugged while they were in Paris in the hope of catching them out in the performance of some loathsome act; but upon their departure he had to admit, sadly, that the only thing to report was that late one night there had been a screaming argument between them and that it seemed one of the young men (it was never clear which) had slapped the other in a hotel lobby.

You can only conjecture what McCarthy and his henchmen would have thought of the events of 1957, when de Gaulle came to power through the fire of Algeria and the subjugation of his own army, when political assassinations were an everyday occurrence and the citizens of Paris were demanding arms to oppose the expected landing of paratroops at Orly. Would the rebellious generals have been considered un-American? un-French? Would the senator and his supporters have been satisfied that death sentences were rare and that even the leader of the underground civil war, General Salan, was spared and later wrote his memoirs for the same house that published the memoirs of his old friend and fellow officer, General de Gaulle? During the period of turmoil, while walking for ten minutes on a street in the eighth arrondissement on the way to dinner, you heard not less than nine explosions as bombs went off in front of the doors of more or less prominent people who had expressed the opinion that perhaps it was time for France to get out once and for all from North Africa. How many members of the Screen Writers' Guild would have lost their jobs for that night's work?

What a holiday Senator McCarthy would have had with an investigation of the *événements* of May 1968, when the students rose and made a battlefield of the Latin Quarter, took over the Sorbonne, called on the working class to rebel, and made poor Jean-Louis Barrault, that gentle and gifted ornament of the French theater, assure the crowd who had noisily invaded his government-subsidized Odéon theater that he was on their side. After which they completely and hideously vandalized the premises and destroyed invaluable stores of scenery and costumes. To complete the circle, M. Barrault was summarily dismissed from his position by Malraux when the shouting died.

Revolutionary slogans were chanted; factories were shut down; obscene cartoons, later to become collectors' items, were everywhere; Maoists, Trotskyites, Stalinists, anarchists, representatives of splinter groups of every shade of the New and Old Left argued and harangued twenty-four hours a day. Original and reasonable demands that had sparked the conflict were forgotten. Blood was shed, families riven, cobbles and tear-gas grenades thrown, barricades erected and stormed in true Parisian fashion. A beautiful baroness, favorably known in the owners' boxes at Longchamp and Deauville, was struck by a policeman's club. A tear-gas grenade was thrown into Régine's, the in-club of Parisian night life, sending several patrons who had certainly never read Marx to the hospital. The car of an English newspaperwoman who was among the most vociferous of the students' apologists was overturned and burned by her brothers and sisters in revolt. The Communist Party made menacing noises but did not move (for fear of American intervention, it was rumored). Mendès-France, once a member of de Gaulle's Cabinet and later Premier of France, marched at the head of a demonstration and as a result brought his political career to an end.

To you as a certain kind of American, it seemed like a senseless and macabre farce. For other Americans, who would have been appalled at the destruction of Washington Square and Greenwich Village by the students of NYU, the insurrection was regarded as a noble crusade, although to this day no one has agreed as to what, exactly, the crusade was about.

At the end, after the tumult subsided and the police returned to their barracks, the students had the satisfaction, if it was indeed a satisfaction, of seeing de Gaulle resign, to be succeeded by Pompidou, hardly a man to warm a student's heart.

You sit at a café, no longer young, comfortably dressed, well-fed, outside that particular struggle, remembering all the generous moments you have witnessed or been a party to that have wound up in absurdity or massacre, and wonder where you would have been, what you would have done during those turbulent days if you had been twenty-one and not yet resigned to the injustice of the world around you.

Mendès-France. He is a friend of yours. Not a close friend. But a friend. He has been to your house. He has invited you to lunch. You admire him. He is a man of principle, intelligence, and courage. You believe that if de Gaulle had heeded his advice and had agreed to declare worthless all the francs printed at the instigation of the Germans during the war, the economy of France would not have gone through the dreadful postwar gyrations of the late forties and early fifties, a time that was characterized all too neatly by a French business acquaintance who, while taking a pre-dinner aperitif, said with a sigh, "Another day in which I have not done one honest thing." The price of survival.

Mendès was not a man to take the easy route out of any situation. In a country where the drinking of wine and consumption of spirits was considered almost a holy rite and a foundation of the economy, he campaigned for sobriety and praised milk, his only drink. And when the bitter task of sweeping up the pieces after the fall of Dien Bien Phu had to be undertaken, it was he, as Prime Minister, who signed the agreement for the withdrawal of the French Army from Indochina. The bitterness he aroused for doing the necessary dirty work was expressed at a wedding party you attended during that period, when a pretty woman, the wife of the mayor of the small town outside Paris who had performed the ceremony, spat out his name contemptuously. "Mendès-France," she said. "He ought to be hanged from the nearest lamppost. Why, he's not even a Frenchman." Her husband, the mayor, hushed her, and someone reminded her that the family of the Prime Minister of France had emigrated from Portugal in the fifteenth century.

At one occasion he was to say, "When de Gaulle finally goes, I am afraid he will leave France with all its institutions destroyed."

Years later, sitting at a café, surrounded by the ex-Prime Minister's prosperous-seeming fellow citizens, you wonder if in the long run his pessimistic prophecy will turn out to be well-founded.

You have dined with Pompidou, too, at the home of Maurice Rheims, one of the leading experts on works of art in France, who conducted auctions for paintings and statues at the Maison Drouot, where collectors from all over the world congregrated on the great days to bid huge sums for the possession of some new treasure that was up for sale. Pompidou was not yet in the government and was still running the Rothschild Bank, and the cares of office had not yet sapped his vitality or charm. He was a handsome man, his face brought brilliantly alive by large, clear, ironic eyes fringed with long, dark, almost girlish lashes. He was the sort of man who was bound to be the center of any gathering, dominating the conversation, enjoying society, speaking with educated assurance in perfect, fluent sentences on whatever subject came up. At the dinner table, at least, he seemed a man much better prepared to run a government than the plodding gentlemen we send to Washington—although you have met many sophisticated Parisians who have envied us our political mediocrities.

After that, Pompidou went on, first to be de Gaulle's Prime Minister and then President of France. Almost certainly, his dinners lost in wit and appetite what they gained in ceremony.

As for the host, M. Rheims, he took the easy way out. Fatigued by the recurring tension of auctioneering—where from time to time he personally had to gamble sums that would have staggered Diamond Jim Brady—he exchanged the gavel and the rostrum for the pen and the desk and became a writer.

Recalling one elegant dinner, you recall others. You remember your first, where a white-gloved butler bent over and whispered in your ear as he poured the wine. Not quite hearing or understanding what the man was saying and fearing that perhaps he was the bearer of a secret, incriminating message, or warning you that your fly was open, you turned and said, *"Pardon, qu'est-ce que vous avez dit?"* Embarrassed now, he spoke a little more loudly. *"J'ai dit, monsieur, Château Lafite, 1929."* Reddening, you hoped that your hostess had not noticed the *gaffe* of her unworldly American guest.

Cruelty, as was to be expected, was not always absent from fashionable gatherings. At one of them, where the gowns of the ladies assembled in the *grand salon* must have cost the seamstresses of the couturiers of Paris thousands of hours with needle and thread, there was a voluptuously built and strikingly handsome lady, the wife of a pushy politician, who wore around her waist a full red sash, tied in a large bow over her magnificently shaped bottom and falling in two blazing streamers behind her. "Ah," noted one of her friends, "she is wearing her Legion of Honor tonight."

Another inveterate diner-out is Maurice Druon, the novelist who won the Prix Goncourt with his first book, joined his uncle, Joseph Kessel, in the Académie Française (and was its youngest member), and later served as Minister of Culture for a brief time—a post in which he distinguished himself by being deplorably frank in a speech in which he addressed himself to the directors of the subsidized theaters of France and said, "Gentlemen, you must not come asking us for money with a begging bowl in one hand and a Molotov cocktail in the other." This perfectly reasonable formula had the result of driving him from the world of politics and back to composing his highly profitable series of books on the kings of France.

His uncle, Joseph Kessel, is a giant of a man, physically and morally, who could at the age of seventy still crush you in his arms when he embraced you after returning from one of his voyages to the far corners of the earth. He accepted the ritual humiliation of campaigning for entrance to the Académie only, as he said, to put to the test his belief in the fundamental integrity of the French intellectual establishment in demanding election of a Jew who was not even born in France. He was a monumentally imposing figure in his green uniform, his leonine head framed by fierce iron-gray hair, his sword at his side, when he stood up to make his first speech under the Coupole. There had been grumbling, of course. One *académicien* had said, "Why Kessel? We already have a Jew—Maurois. And a drunk—Pagnol."

This was more of a *bon mot* than a serious objection. Kessel was a drinker, not a drunk. No drunk could have produced what he has written in his lifetime, astonishing in its volume as well as its variety, unfailing gusto, and sheer qualities ranging, in his novels, from *L'Equipage*—drawn from his experiences as a bombardier in World War I, during which he went on one hundred and sixty missions—through that acute study of perverted Parisian manners, *Belle du Jour,* and the romantic and heroic tale of primitive Afghanistan, *The Horsemen.* His *Army of Shadows,* written out of his experience in the Resistance in World War II, remains the classic of that struggle; his book on the troubles in Ireland reads as though it might have been written by a brilliant Dubliner; and just recently he has published a grim and horrifying account of the Allied intervention in Siberia in 1919, where he served with the French troops on that ill-conceived expedition.

Drunk, indeed. Inevitably it brings to mind the possibly apocryphal anecdote about Abraham Lincoln, who in answer to a complaint that General Grant was a drunk, said, "Find out what brand of whiskey he drinks and I'll send a barrel to all my generals."

So it was with pleasure that, as is the custom in

France, you contributed to the fund, with a host of his other friends, for the purchase of the new *académicien*'s sword and joined him for the long night of celebration after he had made his speech. Less satisfactory was the occasion of the election to the Académie of another of your old friends, Marcel Achard, that charming and humorous man whose comedies were the delight of the Parisian stage for more than forty years and in whose earliest play, *Voulez-Vous Jouer avec Moi?* Beckett might have found some of the inspiration for *Waiting for Godot*.

Once again you made your contribution to the purchase of the sword, again with pleasure. But you had had the misfortune of adapting a great hit of Achard's for the American theater, where it failed, incurring the displeasure of the playwright's wife. Because of that, you could only meet Achard on the sly, and sword or no sword, you were not invited to the party afterward.

It was not as though there was any dearth of parties. There were the huge, dignified June cocktail parties at which the hostesses signed off the end of the social season by inviting some hundreds of their friends and hired policemen, immaculate in white gloves and braided military decorations, to handle the traffic at the door. There were the brawls at James Jones's house on the Ile Saint-Louis, which attracted just about every American living in or passing through Paris—writers, painters, congressmen, racing stable owners, newspapermen, poker players, students, ambassadors, pregnant children in need of advice, editors with a predatory look in their eye, movie producers and directors, ambassadors, enormous touring football players, people hoping for a loan, theatrical ladies, avowed revolutionaries, and assorted representatives of many professions, including the handsome doctor who took care of all American ills in Paris, worried about all our livers, and had to change his telephone number because Elizabeth Taylor or Richard Burton would call him so often in the middle of the night at the first twinge of a headache. There was always something doing in the Jones's living room, with its superb view of the Seine, and it was always amusing. When Jones moved back to the United States, a hollow groan went up from the entire American community in the city.

On the Ile Saint-Louis, too, but high up in a small penthouse from whose terrace you could see the entire sweep of the landscape of Paris, a generous American widow would graciously receive a select group of her friends—most of them, unfortunately, men. When the lady was told by one of her guests that it was impossible that she did not know at least a few young and pretty women, she merely smiled sweetly and said, "Yes. And they're all kept safely in my address book."

If you dined out frequently you would often find yourself at table with that lion of the arts, warfare, and high political controversy, André Malraux, who could be guaranteed to conduct long and instructive monologs on Stalin, Roosevelt, Mao, the history of cats in Egypt, medieval sculpture, de Gaulle, Oriental artifacts, and the internal and external problems of any country you cared to mention.

If you were momentarily surfeited with the pleasures of society, you could drive out with a lady to one of the cozy country inns and, if it was winter, lunch in front of a crackling fire in a room that was so pleasantly decorated that it has been used over and over again as a setting for the movies. In the spring or summer you could be served in the garden, the taste of the cold wine flavored ever so faintly by the scent of flowers, as you joked with the owner, who had told you just after he had opened the small, exquisite hotel, "I have only one rule. Husbands are not permitted to bring their wives."

You sit at the café table staring out at the bare trees and the controlled confusion of the Place de l'Alma, thinking, Perhaps it is better to leave Paris, chuckling softly at the memory of a mischievous little joke as you finish your wine. In the distance, *la Tour Eiffel* rises into the soft gray sky and makes you shake your head, not for the first time, at the peculiar logic of the French language, which puts a phallic symbol of such grandeur into the feminine gender.

You remember how you answered an interviewer who asked why you lived in Paris. "Had Garbo asked you to dinner when you were young," you said, "wouldn't you have gone?"

You close your eyes, shut out the sounds of traffic and café conversation, drift in the realm of memory, float among disconnected images, listen for distant echoes. Things seen, heard, read, remembered, yesterday or ages ago . . .

The clop-clop of the hooves of the horses of the Garde Républicaine trotting past the Square Lamartine on the way to the day's racing in the Bois . . .

The billowing of thousands of bright skirts of the girls on bicycles among the jeeps and command cars on the Champs Elysées at the end of the war . . .

The creak of tumbrils passing through the lanes of

jeering crowds on the way to the guillotine with the victims of the Terror and a king and a queen beheaded . . .

The forlorn sound of horns on the Seine at dawn as the barges push their way down river to Rouen and the Channel, with the newly risen sun reflected in the windows of the Left Bank making it look as though the whole city is in flames . . .

In the hush of a concert hall the city's favorite pianist, Arthur Rubenstein, his fierce, mischievous, ageless face rapt over the keys, strikes the first chords of a Beethoven concerto . . .

In another hall, Piaf chants *La Vie en Rose* and around the corner Montand swings gaily into *Une Demoiselle sur une Balançoire* . . .

Time spirals. The young Picasso arrives from Spain, intent on destroying and rebuilding the structure of contemporary art. Later, when he is an old man, gently reproached by his dealer for the resemblance between his new work and that of Matisse, he says, "But of course. Matisse is dead. Now I must paint for the two of us."

Rimbaud is giving up poetry and leaving for North Africa, Gauguin is packing for his voyage to Tahiti, Radiguet, the brilliant boy, author of *Le Diable au Corps,* is struck by a falling tree on the Champs Elysées and dies at the age of twenty-three . . .

The ladies in black are knocking on a thousand doors to announce that sons and husbands have been killed at Verdun . . .

The heads of State are driving out to Versailles to set up the League of Nations . . .

Gertrude Stein, an angular statue in an historic frieze, survivor of the German Occupation, sits in her living room and plays hostess to the GIs who have discovered her address and throng to her door . . .

James Joyce wanders into the Shakespeare Bookshop on the Place de l'Odéon and cajoles another loan that will never be repaid from the owner of the shop, Sylvia Beach, to help him finish *Ulysses,* then dines at a restaurant which he favors because it is one of the few establishments in the *quartier* that serves Swiss white wine, his preferred tipple. . . .

Hemingway boxes Morley Callaghan in a local gymnasium and is knocked down or not knocked down, according to whose story you believe and visits Fitzgerald and Zelda and takes notes which will be used to grim effect much later, when all three are dead. . . .

The motorists jam the boulevards, honking their horns to the rhythm of *Algérie Française* . . .

Out of the eastern marches of the nation comes the rumbling, like Olympian thunder, of de Gaulle, on television, addressing his countrymen—"Français, Françaises . . ."

You open your eyes, see once more the traffic swirling in the Place de l'Alma, are conscious again of the conversations at the adjoining tables . . .

You try to think of total Paris, that astounding combination of glory and chicanery, of courage and deception, of tolerance and chauvinism, that maelstrom of art and commerce, pleasure and despair, with its fierce republicanism and longing for kings and emperors, and you remember again how Victor Hugo had saluted it with the ringing words, "To have once been Lutèce and to have become Paris—what could be a more magnificent symbol! To have been mud and to have become spirit." You smile a little at the rhetoric, but think, Nobody has said it better than the old man.

You pay your check and rise. The movers and the boys from the American Student Center must have finished and left the empty apartment by now. You will go and say good-bye in English to the owner of the café on the corner. Your bags are packed. As you recross the bridge across the wintry river, you think, I will pick them up, leave the keys for the landlady, and depart.